Chile

Chile

Photos
Hubert Stadler

Text
Susanne Asal

A journey through extremes

B BUCHER

Contents

The sexton of the village church of Parinacota, at an altitude of 4,392 meters (14,409 feet).

Baroque magnificence at the Cerro Santa Lucia in Santiago.

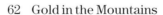

A geological rarity: the granite rocks on the coast near Caldera.

The Tatio geysers in the evening light.

Llaíma Volcano in the Parque Nacional Conguillio.

The daily catch: shellfish from the Magellan Strait.

Did dinosaurs once inhabit the Hurtado Valley?

During the rodeo, the little village
of Chañar in the Hurtado Valley
is transformed into the capital
of the North. Traditionally dressed
in broad-brimmed hats and short
ponchos, huasos like Don Felipe
take part in the contests (above).
Most visitors come to see the
sunsets in the Valle de la Luna
near San Pedro de Atacama. The
photo shows the desert-like Valley
of the Moon during the early
morning. It lies in the Cordillera
de la Sal and originally formed
the bottom of a salar. Erosion
has produced remarkable rock
formations (right).

Spring by Lago Pehoe in the Torres del Paine National Park

> "Behind me, towards the South, the sea
> Has crushed the land
> With its
> Icy hammer…"

Pablo Neruda (1904–1973)

The "Pan de Azucar" National Park, literally "Sugarloaf", lies in **North Chile**. It is easily accessible from Chañaral, the former copper port. It is characterized by **beautiful beaches** and protected species of cactus.

In summer, Papudo is a popular destination for families. The seaside town lies on the coast a short distance north of **Santiago**, and has a long tradition as a holiday resort, as can be seen from the elegant villas lining the beachfront promenade.

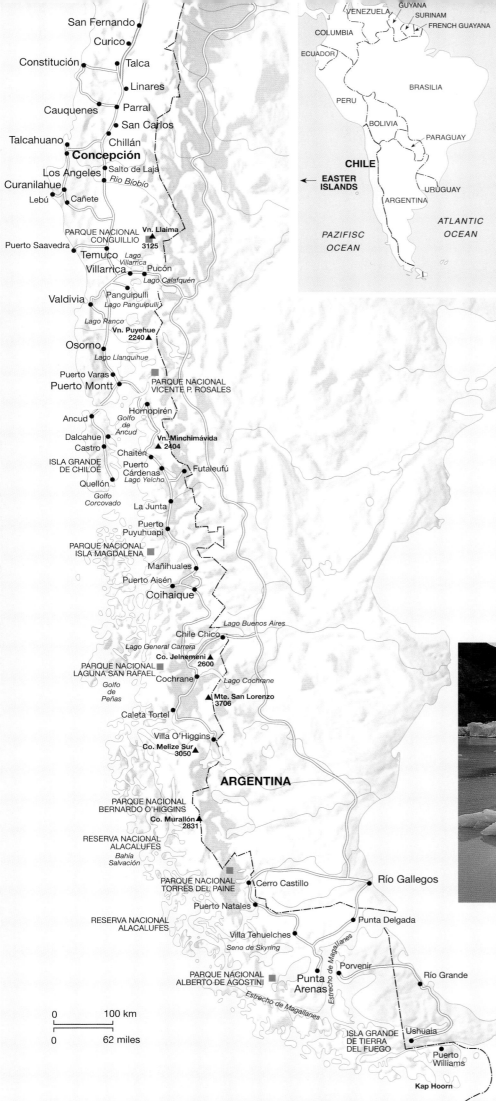

San Fernando
Curico
Constitución
Talca
Linares
Cauquenes
Parral
San Carlos
Talcahuano
Chillán
Concepción
Los Angeles
Salto de Laja
Curanilahue
Río Bíobío
Lebú
Cañete

PARQUE NACIONAL
CONGUILLIO
Vn. Llaima
Puerto Saavedra
3125
Temuco
Lago
Villarrica
Villarrica
Pucón
Lago Calafquén
Valdivia
Panguipulli
Lago Panguipulli
Lago Ranco
Vn. Puyehue
2240
Osorno
Lago Llanquihue
Puerto Varas
Puerto Montt
PARQUE NACIONAL
VICENTE P. ROSALES
Ancud
Hornopirén
Golfo
de
Dalcahue
Ancud
Castro
Vn. Minchimávida
2404
ISLA GRANDE
Chaitén
DE CHILOÉ
Puerto
Futaleufú
Cárdenas
Lago Yelcho
Quellón
Golfo
Corcovado
La Junta
Puerto
Puyuhuapi
PARQUE NACIONAL
ISLA MAGDALENA
Mañihuales
Puerto Aisén
Coihaique
Lago Buenos Aires
Chile Chico
Lago General Carrera
Co. Jelnemeni
PARQUE NACIONAL
2600
LAGUNA SAN RAFAEL
Cochrane
Lago Cochrane
Golfo
de
Peñas
Mte. San Lorenzo
3706
Caleta Tortel
Villa O'Higgins
Co. Melize Sur
3050

ARGENTINA

PARQUE NACIONAL
BERNARDO O'HIGGINS
Co. Murallón
2831
RESERVA NACIONAL
ALACALUFES
Bahía
Salvación
PARQUE NACIONAL
TORRES DEL PAINE
Cerro Castillo
Río Gallegos
Puerto Natales
RESERVA NACIONAL
Punta Delgada
ALACALUFES
Villa Tehuelches
Seno de Skyring
Porvenir
PARQUE NACIONAL
Río Grande
ALBERTO DE AGOSTINI
Punta
Arenas
Estrecho de Magallanes
Estrecho de Magallanes
ISLA GRANDE
Ushuaia
DE TIERRA
DEL FUEGO
Puerto
Williams

Kap Hoorn

0   100 km
0   62 miles

VENEZUELA
GUYANA
SURINAM
COLUMBIA
FRENCH GUAYANA
ECUADOR
BRASILIA
PERU
BOLIVIA
PARAGUAY
CHILE
URUGUAY
EASTER
ISLANDS
ARGENTINA
ATLANTIC
PAZIFISC
OCEAN
OCEAN

The mountains in the background
are already in Argentina:
a lichen-covered monkey-puzzle
tree (araucaria) by Paso Tromen
and Lanin volcano in **South Chile**.

The Grey glacier in the Parque Nacional Torres
del Paine rises in the sea of the same name.
For some years now the glacier in the **Far South**
has been retreating.

The End of the World is Nigh

"Behind me, towards the South, the sea
Has crushed the land
With its
Icy hammer
From the bitter loneliness
Suddenly the silence became an archipelago
And green islands bordered
The waist of my land
Like the pollen or petals
Of a water lily."

Pablo Neruda

Suddenly, the end of the world seems much closer. For Caleta Tortel, for example. The sleepy little village lies among the deep fjords in the south of America, a short distance east of the raging Golfo de Peñas, the "Gulf of Sorrows". Sheltered by vast glaciers and stormy seas, its 508 inhabitants dozed away in their enchanted landscape, until the road destroyed their isolation. Before that, the only way of reaching Caleta Tortel was by boat.

Take your partners! The tango tradition lives on in this café with a dance floor in Bellavista, the lively entertainment district of Santiago (above). – The pilgrimage to the Virgin of Aiquina in the north of the country is an arduous affair. The little town only wakes up at festival time, when it bursts at the seams with exuberant processions and dances. An attractive young Chilean girl shows her national costume (right).

The guanacos have found a safe refuge in the misty Torres del Paine National Park (right-hand page).

The road-construction team had to overcome more than seven mountains to reach the picturesque place slumbering between dense cypress forests and marshes. More than 100 kilometers (63 miles) of rock, swamps, glacial rivers and lakes lay between Caleta Tortel and the next place with a proper road. For a hundred years its inhabitants had lived in isolation in their pretty village which clings to a steep green hillside, entirely built of cypress wood.

The inhabitants of Caleta Tortel arrived here by chance. In 1904 a development company landed in the bay with plans to take over the region, which until then had been inhabited only by snipes, beetles, wolves and the Andean deer known as *huemules*. They declared the region suitable for lumbering and cattle farm-

On the road in Fray Jorge National Park, south of La Serena, the capital of the Norte Chico. The national park, which lies on the coast, possesses a particular microclimate in which rare plants like these cactuses flourish (all photos).

ing. Workers and their families settled here, and merchant ships anchored in the bay. The wood of the magnificent cypress was exported to the north of Chile and even in Europe.

Now those hundred years of solitude are over. Caleta Tortel is now on the map, its coordinates included in the list of places on the beaten track. And 508 Chilean citizens can make their way out into the world, and the world can come to visit them.

How many villages are tucked away like Caleta Tortel or Ollagüe on the Bolivian border in the north, between flamingos, crashing waves, extinct volcanoes and salt crystals in the fjords or the mountains? In Chile, isolation and the need to overcome it have always been an important factor. To this day there are regions as yet unexplored; mountains as yet unseen; tiny islands

upon which no man has yet set foot; mountain lakes, steppes and bays. Caleta Tortel and Ollagüe are just two examples of the way the map of Chile is gradually being filled in.

From Norway to the Sahara

Chile is 4,300 kilometers (2,688 miles) long. This equals the distance between Norway and the Sahara and the range of landscapes the country encompasses is just as varied. Chile's southern coastline has often been compared with the fjord coastline of Norway, for its glaciers, lakes and rivers. Chile may lack the sand dunes of the Sahara, but can actually claim the most arid desert in the world, the Atacama.

Chile's Contribution to the World Heritage

Chiloé has an abundance of more than just nature and seafood: it also has an abundance of churches. The delicate wooden buildings rise skywards above the fields and villages; not a single nail was used in their construction, which is characterized by two- or three-storey belfries and airy arcaded facades. The Jesuit missionaries wanted to create a "Garden of Churches" on Chiloé and its tiny surrounding islets; together with the Franciscans, who arrived some time later, they achieved their aim. More than 150 charming churches and chapels are scattered across the archipelago. They are regarded as outstanding examples of 18th-century wooden architecture. Sixteen of them have been allotted World Heritage status by UNESCO.

The UNESCO list also includes the original and unusual Old Town of Valparaíso, which was added in 2003, and which is regarded as a particularly fine example of port architecture and design during the early globalization period in the 19th century. Chile's first monument to be included in the World Heritage list were the moai, the mysterio us giant statues and the aboriginal culture on Easter Island.

Chileans insist that you must align your bed from north to south, for positioning it from east to west, you risk banging your head on the Andes and finding your feet dangling in the icy sea. They are also convinced that their country, *el último rincón del mundo*, "the farthest corner of the world", has the craziest geography at all.

A bird's eye view of the country can be attained from an aircraft. Chile is a long, narrow country with two almost insurmountable natural boundaries: the Andes in the East, whose highest mountain, Aconcagua, looms above the border between Chile and Argentina; and the Pacific Ocean in the West.

In the North lie the ochre and brownish-red deserts baked by the merciless sun, as well as glittering salt lakes, deeply cut valleys, green and blue lagoons and a world of volcanoes and mountains, colored in every imaginable shade of brown and red. The vegetation is restricted to cactuses, lichens, fungi and small shrubs.

We can see the valleys are conducive to agriculture. Olives, oregano, potatoes, quínoa, carrots, garlic, even flowers flourish and herds of goats are a common sight.

Further south the vegetation becomes more dense, and the Andes rivers provide water for intensely irrigated agriculture. Flying over, the twin mountain ranges of the Andes and the coastal mountains are easy to distinguish and the great valley between. Seen from above, the central and south central regions

look like a gigantic patchwork quilt of fields and towns. The land is cultivated with fruit orchards, vineyards and wheat fields. On the Argentine border, the Andes reach record heights of almost 7,000 meters (23,000 feet); a succession of snow-capped volcanoes stretches out towards the south. Surrounded by dark forests are the lakes that draw so many visitors to Chile.

As the aircraft heads further south, the countryside becomes steadily wilder and more grandiose. Isolated mountain peaks rise up as if carved by a giant hand; the coast is interrupted by countless bays, from time to time seeming like a shattered mirror. Glaciers marbled in shades of blue and silver cover vast tracts of land. The shimmering green of the expanses of forest stretches out as far as the eye can see. Brown stripes leading towards the horizon show where the trees have been cut down. The green, turquoise and azure bays of Lago General Carrera can be clearly made out. In the direction of Argentina, the mountains and forests give way to steppes and terraced uplands *(mesetas)*. The unmistakable peaks of the Torres del Paine soar majestically into the expanse of sky.

The sand on the beaches of the Pan de Azúcar National Park is as soft as velvet, as smooth as silk and the colour of vanilla-flavored sugar (above). – Under the attentive eyes of a flock of pelicans, the fishermen put to sea from the beach at Papudo (bottom left). A shell diver near Caldera prepares his nets for the next catch (bottom right).

See page 24

A Shakespearean fantasy: the lichen forest on Tierra del Fuego.

History in Dates and Pictures

1 A Spanish 8-real silver coin bearing the coat of arms of the King of Spain. – 2 The Indians attacking the Spanish (colored illustration, c. 1550, by Theodor de Bry). – 3 The conquistador Diego Almagro (1475–1538) led the first European expedition to what is now Chile in search of gold. 4 The reconstructed Indio town of Tulor Viejo near San Pedro de Atacama dates from pre-Christian times. – 5 Elected by the people: President Salvador Allende on his way to vote in 1970, surrounded by his followers. – 6 The military junta bombing Moneda Palace on 11 September 1973. President Allende died during the attack. 7 A military putsch brought him to power: General Augusto Pinochet. 8 Eduardo Frei Ruiz-Tagle, Second President of the Concertación between 1994–2000.

The oldest archeological finds show that Chile has been inhabited since the 13th millennium B.C. The Atacameños were migrants from the North who settled beside the rivers in the mountain oases of the Andes.

The Chinchorro culture, which expanded across the river oases of Lluta and Azapa, left traces around what is now Arica. The oldest mummies in the world, which can be examined in the museum of San Miguel de Azapa, are estimated to be 9,000 years old.

The Chango settled the northern coastal strip. They were whale hunters and built boats of sealskin. The territory of the Tehuelche lay in the deep south of the country. One of the caves which they used for cult purposes has recently been discovered near Villa Cerro Castillo on Lago General Carrera.

The Alacalufes lived in the labyrinth of fjords and islets; further south, between the Beagle Channel and Cape Horn, lay the home of the Yamana. The Selk'nam hunted guanacos on Tierra del Fuego.

From the first millennium B.C. the land was more densely settled by tribes which came across the Andes from what is now Northwest Argentina. The Tihuanaco culture brought the first Golden Age to the north of the country; its roots lay by Lake Titicaca, situated between Bolivia and Peru. The Diaguita, who became famous for their pottery, settled near what is now La Serena. From 1470 Chile was conquered by the Incas, who advanced as far as the Río Maule. Only one tribe refused to submit itself to their rule: the Mapuche, who retreated beyond the Río Biobío.

They also fought bitterly against the armies of Spanish conquistadors, who arrived from 1540 under Pedro de Valdivia. Augustinian, Franciscan and Dominican monks as well as Jesuits arrived in the wake of the conquistadors, founding the first university in Santiago in 1747.

As elsewhere on the subcontinent, towards the end of the 18th century resistance grew to the exploitation by the mother country. The

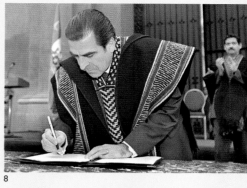

ment put a bloody end to the experiment. Under the following military dictatorship of Augusto Pinochet, freedom of speech was buried and the country's economic problems treated with remedies from the neo-liberal box of tricks. In 1988 the majority of Chileans voted against an extension of Pinochet's term in office. After 16 years of military dictatorship, Chile became once more a republic headed a president. The first presidential elections were won by Christian Democrat P. Aylwin, the candidate nominated by the opposition alliance *Concertación de Partidos por la Democracia* (CPPD). During his term of office Chile's democratization made considerable progress. Thanks to its successful economic policy, the CPPD was victorious again in the parliamentary and presidential elections in December 1993. It was only in 2006 that the Socialists, under their leader, Michelle Bachelet, succeeded in taking over. Chile's modern industry and well-developed service sector have transformed the country's economy into one of the most productive on the Latin American subcontinent, as well as the world's biggest exporter of copper.

citizens of Chile demanded representation and a liberalization of the economy. Chile gained its independence in 1818 under the military leadership of Bernardo O'Higgins.

A period of confusion on the political scene was ended by the conservative, authoritarian Diego Portales in 1830, who pandered to the interests of the farming and trading oligarchy. With the beginning of industrialization, the country became increasingly urbanized. After winning the War of the Pacific, in 1884 Chile gained the Bolivian and Peruvian provinces of Antofagasta and Tarapacá. In the meantime, the expulsion of the Mapuche and colonization by European, mostly German, immigrants, continued apace under presidents Manuel Bulnes and Manuel Montt.

Political instability dogged Chile into the 20th century. Industrial workers founded the Socialist Workers' Party in 1912. Populist governments with social democratic policies alternated with more right-wing groups. Women acquired the vote in 1949.

The most momentous period of Chilean history began when the socialist Salvador Allende Gossens became President in 1970. The hopes of the entire subcontinent for a left-wing socialist renewal rested on him. The U.S. govern-

21

1

Hoornse Eylandt
Isle de Hoorn

2

3

22

5

6

4

1 View of Valparaíso (Painting
by Johann Moritz Rugendas,
c. 1835/50). – 2 A Dutch ship on the
coast of the Tierra del Fuego Indians,
with Cape Horn in the background
(Illustration from a 17th-century
travelogue). – 3 View of Valparaíso
(Photograph, c. 1920). – 4 Hunting
wild llamas near Antuco volcano
(chalk lithograph, c. 1850).
5, 6 Valparaíso (Engraving, c. 1850
and photograph, c. 1960).

23

Gusts of wind make landing in Punta Arenas seem hazardous, but the pilot merely smiles; such weather is normal here, and he has been trained to cope. With nothing in its way the wind sweeps mightily across the steppes of Magellanes and Tierra del Fuego.

The Founding of the Country

Even seen from an aircraft from a distance, one thing is clear: the natural conditions represent a challenge for aspiring settlers. For many years, chance dictated where and how the country was developed. An infrastructure was only built up in those regions where it was required for strategic-political or economic reasons. During colonial times, Chile's borders were not yet fixed, nor was

there an overall settlement plan. After independence in 1818, the most important tasks facing the settlers were to give the country a structure and to secure the borders.

The young state of Chile was neither able nor willing to undertake this exercise alone. The results were not always to the country's advantage. During the 19th century, the period during which the country was established, the government allowed adventurers, pioneers and businessmen every freedom as they built up the country, exploited its resources and took them for themselves – cattle farming, mining and timber. A skeleton railway system, road network and village structures arose for the benefit of the population at large, waiting to be taken over and extended.

The result was often unfair ownership ratios, which harbored the danger of development inequality. Pioneers asked for land and were granted it, but if a more powerful company appeared on the scene and promised development across a larger area, the small farmers would often find themselves at a disadvantage. South of Coyhaique, entire regions changed hands in this way.

The map of Chile still reflects this unequal development and the struggles arising from the time when the land was being developed and made agriculturally viable. In the north, the cemeteries along the Panamericana recall the nameless dead who were killed in the nitrates extraction camps. In the south, you will drive past hundreds of miles of dead forests and bleached tree stumps, bearing witnesses to the time when slash-and-burn was implemented in an attempt to tame the jungle.

Apart from the powerful Mapuche tribe, the original inhabitants of Patagonia are virtually extinct. The Tehuelche, Selk'nam,

Alacalufes and Yamana tribes, to name only the most famous Indian peoples, survived the Spanish conquistadors but not the young Chilean nation. Just eight Alacalufes still live in their last refuge, Puerto Edén, which sits like a tiny dot between the immense fjords and islands of the deep South.

During the 1880s the Portuguese and Irish sheep farmers of Tierra del Fuego hunted the Selk'nam people and paid their killers according to the number of severed ears which they delivered. The nomadic tribes upset their plans to turn the millions of hectares of land they had been granted by the state into lucrative sheep pasture. The cruel murder of the Indians recalls the campaigns against the original inhabitants of North America. Museums in Porvenir, Puerto Williams and especially the Salesian monastery in Punta Arenas document the destruction of Chile's original inhabitants.

Roads into Nothingness

Today it is the state which is responsible for the development of the country. The original relationships have been reversed. The construction of the Carretera Austral, the road which runs through the glacial fields of the South, was begun by the military under Pinochet in 1986, in order to provide better access to remote settlements. That, at least, is the official version. Hamlet by hamlet, farm by farm, hundreds of miles apart, they were linked together like beads on a necklace. The bold project is due for completion some time during the next decade. The democratic government continues to send civil engineers and military personnel on road-building projects to places like Caleta Tortel.

The Chilean nation has thrown itself into the business of setting up networks in other ways, too. Members of the national organization ESA, which is responsible for bringing the necessary supplies to remote regions, crawl out of their jeeps covered in dust or stagger nauseously out of ferries stinking of kerosene as they bring the coveted goods to inaccessible settlements: peas, wire, nails. The Senderos de Chile, a network of footpaths, will one day criss-cross the entire length of the country from Visviri on the Bolivian border to Tierra del Fuego.

There is a great deal to discover in Chile. Time and again, surprising new treasures are brought to light and studied. For example the petroglyphs near Arica and the Indian fortresses in the far North, or the pre-Hispanic rock paintings near Villa Cerro Castillo, produced by the Tehuelche and estimated to be more than 10,000 years old. Or the discovery that dinosaurs lived up

See page 30

German immigrants once settled in Puerto Octay, (above). – Right-hand page: Aiquina comes to life during the pilgrimage to the Virgin of Guadalupe (top). – Bars in San Pedro de Atacama (center). – Market at Parinacota (bottom left) and a shell merchant on Chiloé.

Sea Urchins and Indian Cuisine

Surprising Specialities on Chile's Plates

1 A pleasant surprise: in the restaurant of the Hotel "José Nogueira" in Punta Arenas, the grapes grow on the pergola.
2 In the "Azul Profundo" in Bellavista in Santiago, everyone loves Pablo Neruda and seafood.
3 In the kitchen of one of the best restaurants in South Chile: the "Merlin" in Puerto Varas.
4 An exclusive Andalusian setting provides the background for elegant dining: the famous "Centro Español" in Iquique. – 5 "El otor Loco": behind the graffiti, top-quality fish dishes are served (bottom right).
6.–8. Chops, empanadas (filled pasta) and fish stew are everyday dishes in Chile.

In Chile, any seafood fan will face a challenge: raw sea urchin. Not everyone succumbs to the temptation. Chileans love their *erizos*. They drizzle lemon juice or white wine on the white flesh before swallowing it.

Many have no qualms about eating raw seafood. *Mariscal* is a mixed raw seafood platter including oysters, scallops and the bright orange-red *piure*, as well as sea urchin. For more sensitive stomachs there is a cooked version, *paila marina*, which also includes mussels and abalone, known in Chile as *loco*.

With its 6,435 kilometers (4,022 miles) of coastline it is not surprising that the main ingredients of Chile's national cuisine come from the sea. Pable Neruda even wrote an ode to the conger eel, *congrio*. They form the basis for soups such as "Luna y Miel", the "Honeymoon Soup" made of mussels and *picorocos*, which are grilled with garlic or covered with a mixture of parsley, chilli and oil *(pil-pil)*. A light cream sauce of shrimps and mussels accompanies fish *(salsa marinera)*. Swordfish *(albacora)* or sea bass *(robalo)* taste best when freshly prepared on a grill *(plancha)*. The most expensive dish in Chile is the bright red *centolla*, the Southern King Crab, costing approx. $ 100 and tasting like lobster.

Chileans abroad miss the *centolla* less than the sandwiches, which are served in great variety in *sandwicherias*. Grilled or roast beef or

28

6

7

8

chicken fillet is piled between two halves of a roll, covered with melted cheese (the invention of former president Barros Luco, it is said),

and then with onions and lettuce or slices of avocado or tomato. If you order a *completo*, you will get a hot dog; "complete" means with a garnish of ketchup, mayonnaise and mustard. Alternatively you can munch a crisp *empanada* from the oven, often filled with a mixture of mincemeat, hard-boiled egg, olives, raisins and Arabian spices. The national dish of the central region also reflects the

tastes of Arabia: the corn cake pastel del *choclo* is actually savory, but flavored with honey and a pinch of cardamom.

The origins of *cazuelas* lie in Indian cuisine. The stews made of beef or chicken with carrots, potatoes, corn, pumpkin and *cilantro* taste best in the Andes. Quinoa, a type of cereal, is ground into flour by the Aymara and made into cookies, cakes and pies.

The position is clear when it comes to the favorite Chilean meal with guests: *asado*.

Cooking may generally be women's work, but when it comes to grilling, no self-respecting man would allow his Señora anywhere near the fire.

The guests feast on steaks, fillets and sausages with salads. The party continues until the meat has all been eaten.

29

Huasos at home: at the horse races in Cochamó (center) and at the Hacienda Los Andes in the Valle Hurtaod (left).

near the highest volcano in the world and the highest mountain in Chile, the Ojos del Salado. Or that, in the vicinity of Puerto Ibáñez on Lago General Carrera, burial sites of the first inhabitants are hidden away beneath the hills which look like heaps of stones to the unschooled eye.

During the past two decades, there has been a veritable flood of nominations of cities and buildings as UNESCO World Heritage monuments or as part of the Patrimonio Cultural Nacional, the National Cultural Heritage. The UNESCO list includes Easter Island (1995), the churches on the Isla de Chiloé (2000) and the historic center of Valparaíso (2003), which is regarded as a particularly fine example of port architecture and design during the early globalization period in the 19th century. Chile's first monument to be included in the World Heritage list were the moai, the mysterious giant statues and the aboriginal culture on Easter Island.

From the abandoned railway station in Arica to the nitrate offices in Humberstone and Laura to the typical landscapes of Caleta Tortel and the center of Punta Arenas, the protected sites, buildings and industrial complexes are spread out across the entire land. They bear witness to a tumultuous past which the country is gradually beginning to re-discover and to value.

The Latin American Tiger

Today, Chile likes to present itself as a cosmopolitan country. On Sundays the *santigueños*, as the inhabitants of the capital call themselves, go picnicking, walking or swimming on San Cristóbal hill. Below them, the city sprawls at their feet. The rich and poor districts disappear in the dusty summer haze, and the entire city looks like a box of building bricks from a jeweler's shop. The

Chileans are particularly proud of the gleaming, brightly-colored, post-modern blocks as they stand lined up beside each other. Today the architecture of the inner city is playful, almost trendy. It symbolizes the country's progress, a role which the country has played convincingly and to good effect within its Latin-American context for more than a decade. Chile is the most important economic power on the continent, the Latin American "tiger". In fact, Chile's economy is both stable and crisis-resistant; it is currently profiting from the fact that the price of copper has reached a new high. Chile supplies 36 percent of the world market with the metal.

If you stroll through the streets of the Providencia district you will find yourself, just like anywhere else in the world, treading the stamping ground of the "young urban professional." You will need no help to find your way around here: mobile telephone

at the ready, dark suit, big-city bustle, Business-Lunch menus in little restaurants, shopping malls. The latest trend is for sparkling wine and wine to be served by the glass and not just by the bottle – a new fad which has been greeted with enthusiasm by the glossy gourmet magazines. Please note: a Chilean yuppie would not be seen dead with a proletarian glass of beer.

The current generation of 30 to 40-year-olds is coasting along on the latest wave of globalization. They have heard far too much about the dictatorship and Pinochet and the socialist experiment of Dr. Salvador Allende. Above all, they do not wish to be associated with such things.

It is possible that the country still harbors plenty of *pinochistas*, but they are old and are dying out. To the younger generation they are simply old fossils holding up the wheel of progress, like sand in a gearbox. A dictatorship is not modern, and in any case maybe we have forgotten that, bar one, Chile was never ruled by a dictatorship. And that was a historical error. That is the opinion today.

In establishment circles you will hear praise for the misunderstood Allende, a martyr to his cause, and the neo-liberal restructuring of the economy under Pinochet; no one sees these opposing viewpoints as contradictory. In any case, the socialist

Ricardo Lagos is doing a good job. He is the most successful president of the Concertación, the coalition of originally 16 different political parties which took over after Pinochet. During the first two legislative periods it was led by Christian Democrats. In the colorful world of young (business) people there is a place for everything.

A forest of myrtles beside Lago Riesco near Puerto Aisén (left-hand page). The bay of Caleta Tortel has only recently become accessible by car (center). – The prosperity of Caleta Tortel is based on cypress wood (top right). Church on the Carretera Austral (center right).

The Lagos government also knows the political answers to the pressing social problems and the sale of natural resources (fish, wood) to foreign firms, long an important economic factor but currently showing reduced demand.

Across the centuries, Chile could claim to be *el último rincón del mundo*, the farthest corner of the world, in more senses than one. Now we are slowly beginning to take possession of that farthest corner. Like Caleta Tortel, with its unique stairways and jetties of cypress wood. Like Colchane, surrounded by the glittering salt flats. And like the inimitable Chilean forest.

"... deep and dark
Were the forests,
Luminous with glow worms
The mud phosphorescent,
The trees had long ropes hanging down
Like in a circus,
And the light sprang from drop to drop
Like a green dancer in the thicket."

Pablo Neruda

33

*The hanging glacier of Queulat
lies surrounded by dense forests in
the south of Chile. Several
footpaths lead to the base of the
glacier (above). – The peaks of the
Grey glacier shimmer like
imprisoned light in shades of
azure blue (right).*

34

The Laguna Santa Rosa against the Ojos del Salado.

Communion Wine as an Export Winner

Chile's Vineyards on the Road to Success

1

2

3

4

1, 2, 4 The liquid gold is stored in the Santa Carolina winery in Santiago.
3. In the Valle del Elqui the land is covered with espalier-trained Pisco vines.
6 In the manor house of the Santa Carolina Winery.
5 and 7 Pisco, the national drink of Chile, is distilled from the Pisco grape in the Elqui Valley.

The West Indies had been discovered, the New World put on the map and Pope Alexander VI had ordered that the original inhabitants be converted to Christianity. And the priests, who had followed the conquistadors into the unknown wilderness, had a problem. How were they to celebrate the transubstantiation, the central part of any Catholic mass, with no wine to symbolize the Blood of Christ?

As there were no grapes in Latin America, they had to be imported from the Old World. And so a decree was promulgated in Seville in 1564, stating that every ship setting sail for the West Indies was to carry on board a supply of vines. Later the monastic orders which ran the monasteries took their own vines with them. And so wine was introduced to Chile. It is no longer known exactly where the first vineyard was planted but it is estimated to have been near Santiago or Concepción. To this day the irrigation of the vineyards still follows the order of the ancient Inca canal system.

Although we can assume that the enjoyment of wine in Chile was not the sole prerogative of the clergy, nonetheless initially viticulture played only a minor role in the development of the country. País, a muscatel grape, was planted. In the mid-19th century, when the burgeoning new middle class had made fortunes in the mining industry a fashion emerged for cultivating vineyards and things changed rapidly. Rich families imported French grape varieties like Merlot,

38

5

7

5

6

smells of melon, peach and honey, the Carmenère of tobacco and leather. Today, all French noble grape varieties are represented on Chilean soil, from Pinot Noir to Semillon.

The main wine-growing regions surround the Central Zone and stretch as far as the Andes. The most famous are the valleys of the Maipo and Curico, in which you will find more velvety, woodland accents, including the Colchagua valley to the South, which produces fresher accents tinged with citrus. The varieties grown in Valle Casablanca near the coast have a particularly lively taste because the Pacific night mists "close" the vines.

The further north you travel, the more rounded the wines become. Around La Serena they develop a peppery aroma. The red wines from Tarapacá are rich and taste of wood and tannin.

In future, vines are to be planted as far south as Concepción, in order to introduce yet another type of wine. A proper German Riesling may well be the result.

Cabernet, Sauvignon and Chardonnay and all flourished in their new surroundings. Many vineyards bear family names: Cousiño Macul or Undurraga, or are named after a saint: Santa Emiliana, Santa Rita.

Today the wine is by no means exclusively for family consumption. Chilean wine is conquering the world market – justifiably, according to the experts, although there is still no system for confirming its region of origin (DOC) as in Europe.

In fact, that will soon change. The climate is ideal for the dry summers discourage pests, and glacial rivers supply necessary minerals.

The aromas of Chilean white wines explode with exotic-fruity flavours. The popular Chardonnay

Where Chile was Born

Santiago and Surroundings

Whenever Heredia, the private detective, skulks through the Calle Bandera in his trench-coat with his eyes half-closed, you can be certain that he has drunk a little more than was strictly necessary to quench his thirst. His girl friend has probably left him and he is having problems solving his latest case. Life is not at all easy for the sleuth, who frequently loses sight of his trail in newly globalized Santiago with its chic yuppie districts El Bosque Norte and Las Condes. Heredia belongs to the old school and lives appropriately

There is a magnificent view of the sea from the terrace of the "Café Turri" in Valparaíso (above). – The sky-blue Edificio Edwards on the Plaza de Armas in Santiago harks back to the Belle Époque in Paris. Today it is a department store (right-hand page).

A young Chilean girl in Viña del Mar.

enough between the prostitutes and workers in the old center of the Chilean capital, where the facades grow ever paler and the pavements more full of potholes.

Private detective Heredia was created by the Chilean writer Ramón Díaz Eterovic. He inhabits a twilight world between drugs, honest emotions, deceived women and loyal policemen. They all live somewhere in a Chilean no-man's land as it redefines itself economically and politically.

In the Heart of the City

Heredia, the melancholy private detective, loves the Santiago of the good old days, and the traditions which are still lived out on the Plaza de Armas. In spite of its belligerent name – "Munitions Square" –, which it shares with all central squares throughout Chile, the Plaza de Armas remains the heart of the historic capital. Part of the square has been sacrificed to two new vehicle

lanes, but that does not detract from the atmosphere. Admittedly the cream-colored music kiosk now lies somewhat grotesquely on the very edge of the square. But the entire team continues to gather here, and to find ready customers: portrait painters, shoe cleaners, newspaper sellers and photographers who take holiday snapshots. Old-fashioned wrought-iron benches provide the seating needed to recover from the midday sun. The fountains and trees are still here. Even today locals insist that Santiago's learn either to walk or eat ice cream on the Plaza de Armas – both if they are lucky.

But society is changing, and with it the city's countenance. In line with its new identity as South America's top economic powerhouse, an attractive new center has emerged further to the East. The charming, old-fashioned appearance of Old Santiago, by contrast, looks like a slightly down-at-heel version of some European capital.

This comes as no surprise as capitals of the New World always took their architectural inspiration from European origins across the ocean. Both Buenos Aires and Lima bear this out incontestably. Santiago welcomed large numbers of European immigrants and the wealthy left their mark on the city, their home country providing the main architectural input. Two main thoroughfares, currently being renovated, were even christened "Barrio Paris – Londres."

A Stroll through the City's History

If you climb the Cerro Santa Lucía in the city center, you can look down onto the glittering facades of modern Santiago (center), which dwarf the historic buildings around the Plaza de Armas (top and bottom).

In Santiago, the capital of the "Farthest Corner of the World", tucked away beyond the Andes, the citizens enjoyed a promenade just as their counterparts in Paris or Madrid. The Plaza de Armas was a popular rendezvous. The Avenida Bernardo O'Higgins is the city's main thoroughfare to this day. The tree-lined avenue was favored by prosperous citizens, taking a stroll or a drive to showing off their fashionable clothes or carriages – or both. If you ignore today's exhaust fumes and the loud traffic noise to take a second look at its layout, the historic intent becomes clear. In the middle, a strip of grass planted with trees separates the carriageways; on either side, you will spot here and there the odd, slightly dilapidated palazzo.

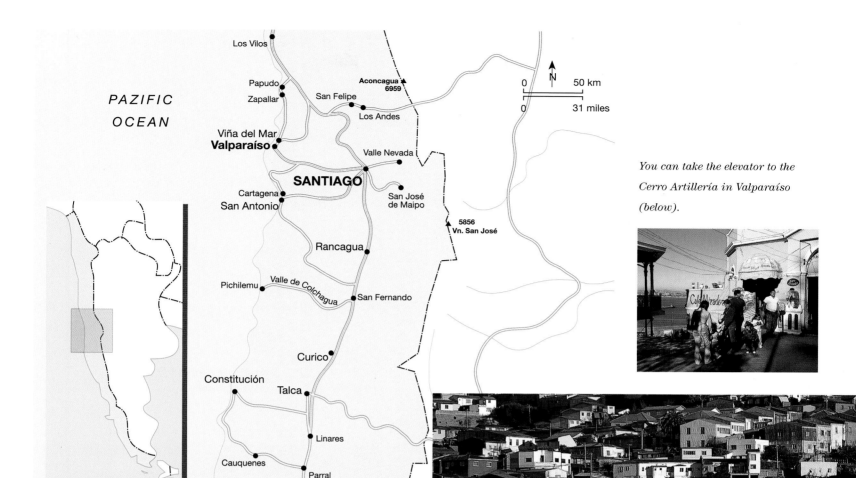

You can take the elevator to the Cerro Artillería in Valparaíso (below).

In order to get the best view of the brightly colored "shoe-box" architecture of Valparaíso, the town on a thousand hills, you should climb up and down the stairways surrounding the bay (center). – The sandy beach at Papudo – a sophisticated Belle Époque seaside resort (left).

Let us take a stroll through Mr Heredia's inner city. There is plenty to see, for it is the focal point of the so-called city of the 1940s, as can be seen from the Art-Déco architecture in the Calle Nueva York, for example, in which the pillared façade of the Stock Exchange building soars upwards like the "Titanic." Nearby is the Plaza de la Constitución featuring what was once the royal mint, a neo-classical palazzo called La Moneda, which has been used as the seat of government and presidential headquarters since 1958.

The city's period of expansion produced buildings with massive, decorated stone façades which have determined Santiago's countenance.

The main post office building, the villas built for the patrician Errázuriz, Cousiño and Aritzía families, wrought-iron constructions, arcades and old department stores. Crowded between are bustling pedestrian areas where street traders have set up their stalls.

The ground floors of those grand family villas are now occupied by brightly painted self-service drugstores or the "El Pollo Feliz" fast-food chain. The Chinese offer cheap goods "Todo por

43

An attractive palace for housing the fine arts: the Museo de Bellas Artes in Santiago (above). The fountain in front of the Teatro Municipal in Santiago (top right). Large sections of the historic center have been transformed into pedestrian zones (right).

cien", everything for 100 pesos, and street traders energetically advertise their wares defending their patch with T-shirts, ballpoint pens, bath towels and maps. And they all try to persuade the average Chilean that he hasn't really got much money in his pocket.

Two other institutions in the city center do not compete with each other in any way. In the cafés "Haiti" und "Caribe", curvaceous ladies in extremely short skirts serve espressi to elderly gentlemen; whilst in the "Café Colonia" staff decorate meter-high gâteaux with whipped cream. For decades the latter has defended its position as a city-center institution and is proud of its traditional German cake recipes. The cafés con piernas, the "cafés with legs," as they are known here, target a very different clientele.

The Stomach of Santiago

Is there a better place for the "Stomach of Santiago" than this district of the city? Gentle light filters through a delicate glass and steel dome across the pyramids of fruits and fish in the Mercado Central food market. All the ingredients needed for a fine lunch can be found here. Freshly caught fish and seafood are a must. Nobody here objects to the copious use of garlic. Cognoscenti drink camomile tea as a digestif.

Following that, you have to cross the Río Mapocho. On the other side of the river is Bellavista, the city's hippie-bohemian-artistic-advertising agency-entertainment district. The residents live in brightly painted houses. Here, too, you will find one of the houses of Pablo Neruda (1904-1973).

The poet had supported and subsequently was banned under Pinochet Salvador Allende's election campaign. He was an ambassador for Chile under various governments and also won the Nobel Prize for Literature in 1971. In the 1990s he became rehabilitated in his home country. The poet had supported Salvador Allende's election campaign and subsequently was banned under the dictator Pinochet. He was an ambassador for Chile under various governments and also won the Nobel Prize for Literature in 1971. In the 1990s he finally became rehabilitated in his home country and is considered one of the main representatives of Latin America's literature. After the floods and destruction under the military regime, Neruda's houses in Santiago, Valparaíso and Isla Negra – all places which no doubt Heredia would have liked – have been rebuilt and restored. The witty ensembles of stacked circular buildings, lookout towers and labyrinthine interiors are now some of the most attractive museums in the country. Visitors love to see Neruda's unusual collection of figureheads (including masculine ones!) as well as his circus horses and stuffed horses.

Ten Cottages Achieve World Fame

Readers who are familiar with his poems will not be surprised to discover that Pablo Neruda loved Valparaíso. The town lies beside the sea, 120 kilometers (75 miles) from Santiago. Pedro de Valdivia, the founder of Santiago, determined in 1542 that the bay should serve as an anchorage and trading port, but it was some time before Valparaíso developed into that role. In the early years, just ten cottages and a church waited in vain for company. Callao in Peru was the Spanish colony's main port and all business with Spain came through its waters. Spain's centralist economic policy forbade the individual colonies to trade with each other, and as a result subsidiary ports had no way of developing. Valparaíso remained very small.

The elegant interior of the Santiago Stock Exchange (above). The atmosphere in this restaurant is equally grand (right). – The Plaza de Armas, the historic center of Santiago, is bustling with people eating, drinking, playing and discussing with each other animatedly (right-hand page).

Expansion came with independence and trade increased. The route between Europe and America led round Cape Horn or through the Magellan Strait. Valparaíso was the first port at which sailing vessels and steamships could anchor, discharge their freight and reload, after rounding the horn and it soon thereafter became an important base for trading companies.

The ten cottages grew into a proper town which quickly spread out across the cordillera which rises steeply from the coast.

See page 52

Ricas Empanadas
de Horno Ravera

Santiago de Chile

The most picturesque walk

1 A bustling metropolis: Tourists and businessmen crowd the pedestrian areas. – 2 The Mapuche monument on the Plaza de Armas. 3 From the summit of the Cerro San Cristóbal, which you can reach by rack and pinion railway, you will have the city at your feet. 4 Street traders against a historical backdrop: Santiago Railway Station. – 5 Modern art is displayed in the historic setting of the Museo de Bellas Artes. – 6 Whiter than white: the Immaculate Conception statue on the Cerro San Cristóbal.

Our walk begins beside Santa Lucía, a hill in the center of Santiago which looks as if it has broken off from the coastal mountain chain. Baroque staircases, paths and terraces provide a framework for the luxuriant vegetation. Atop the hill stands an old fort built in 1816 to defend the Spanish their territorial claims. The Mapuche named it Huelén, "Suffering."

On a sunny summer day, it is a pleasure to amble beneath the shady trees. On warm evenings concerts and theatrical performances are staged on the terraces. The National Library, built in 1924, one of the largest in South America, was at the foot of Cerro Santa Lucía.

Stretching eastward, the Avenida O'Higgins was a grand boulevard

designed in the 19th century. now-popularly known as Alameda. It is the main traffic thoroughfare forming a backbone determining the city center's structure.

Three blocks on, the Paseo Ahumada forks off to the right. The faded beauty of a succession of shopping arcades tells us that the Paseo was the fashionable shopping area of the 1920s.

A detour to the west along Agustinas leads to the Plaza de la Constitución and the ornate Renaissance façade of La Moneda, the former

mint which since 1958 has been the seat of government. Before it is a statue in honor of President Salvador Allende, who was killed there in 1973 when the building was bombed during the military putsch.

Around the Plaza de Armas, the green lung of old Santiago, are

6

5

grouped the Cathedral and its Museum of Religious Art, the Portal Fernández Concha featuring the legendary restaurant "Chez Henry" beneath its arches, and the pastel-colored neo-classical Central Post Office, next door to the Palacio de la Real Audiencia. Its present-day appearance – a mixture of neo-classical elements – dates from 1846 and it now functions as the Natural History Museum.

The city administration occupies the palazzo next door. The City museum is located in a deep-red palazzo one belonging to a Spanish grandee in Calle Merced on the south-east border of the Plaza de Armas. The charming Museum for Pre-Colombian Art (Calle Bandera) is situated in the colonial-style Royal Customs House beyond the Plaza d'Armas.

To the north, on the banks of the Mapocho is the Estación Mapocho, a decorative railway station which nowadays is the setting for exhibitions and concerts. Diagonally opposite, behind a row of nondescript fast-food stalls is the food market and here you can eat the freshest seafood every day (including Sundays!)

The Parque Forestal runs alongside the river. It is a well-kept park dotted with monuments. To the east the is situated the Museo de Bellas Artes, a monumental 19th-century building exhibiting fine art as well as the Contemporary Art Museum.

Heading back again, you will come across the Calle Lastarría to the south. The little Plaza Mulato Gil de Castro and its the Archeological Museum is an oasis of peace and tranquility.

49

The marvellous seaside resort of Zappalar near Santiago.

"Late at night, the Beagle anchored in the bay of Valparaíso, the main port of Chile. In the light of dawn it all looked very charming. After Tierra del Fuego the climate felt delightful – the atmosphere was so dry and the sky so clear and blue and the sun shone brightly, so that the all of nature seemed bursting with life. The anchorage is very pretty. The town is built directly at the foot of a steeply rising mountain chain about 1,600 feet high," noted Charles Darwin in his diary on 23 July 1833, later to become the literary sensation entitled "The Voyage of the Beagle."

Everyone who sees the town agrees that it cannot have been easy to build on this site, which resembles an amphitheater. The inhabitants, architects and builders solved the problem with such originality the town centre is on the UNESCO World Heritage list meaning Valparaíso is officially regarded as one of the most picturesque towns in the world.

"Paradise Valley" is a town made for walking. Its steep, narrow alleys and precipitous districts are linked by an assortment of stairways and passages. Where the foundations are too steep elevators and cable cars come into operation, some of them over 100 years old. All this naturally adds to the town's fascination. Valparaíso is vibrant. Its unique historic character and its exceptional appearance is not just derived from its numerous renovated palazzi and captains' villas, but also from the slightly scruffy port and market districts and typically brightly colored houses. No one, of course, would expect a port to radiate a sterile beauty.

Neruda's house here is perched like a nest above a steep slope. His third residence is in Isla Negra, the "Black Island". No island actually, but a wooded coastal resort framed by black rocks. It attracts a constant stream of visitors, and you have to reckon with waiting periods for the crossing and house tour.

Popular beaches and tourist bunkers are always in fashion, and Chile is no different. Viña del Mar, Valparaíso's sister city, is a villa suburb joined to the main city by a five-kilometer-long (three

Valparaíso: the very name evokes visions of faraway places. – Built around a dramatic bay, the historic center of the old port has recently been included in the list of UNESCO World Heritage sites (above). – On the Plaza Sotomayor (below).

miles) urban motorway. It has popular beaches, the highlight being Reñaca, which is also a must for fitness freaks. A hint of irony does not come amiss in Viña del Mar: it is the traditional venue of the South American Pop Festival, which is staged every year in February, and is also the stage of the "Festival d'Cebolla,", the "Onion Festival" for the sub-continent's kitschiest tear-jerkers. They, too, find a ready audience. Cognoscenti maintain that all participants could just as well enter – and win – either category.

The Countryside

What did this densely populated centre of the country previously look like? As far as we know, Chile had few inhabitants when the Spanish arrived, since the soil was not very fertile. The flat land was covered with scrub, and only the region at the foot of the Andes had more luxuriant vegetation. The Spanish immediately divided the land between themselves and enslaved the Indios. Initially the Spanish dug for gold only later discovering the soil fertile enough for agriculture. They replaced the Indian crops of maize, quínoa and potatoes with wheat. Later cattle, sheep and pigs were introduced and the eradication of all Indian traditions was complete.

The wheat met with a ready market. Following independence in 1818, California expressed interest and later, Australia. Areas of cultivation were extended, forests destroyed, and irrigation canals dug to increase productivity. Aside from the towns which

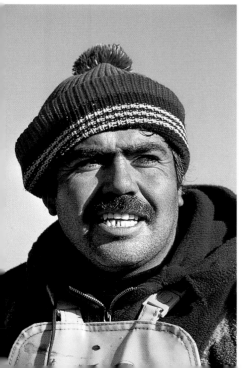

grew up the landscape still looks much the same today as it did then. Chile's granary stretches between Rancagua, 80 kilometers (50 miles) south of Santiago, Chillán famous for its fruit and vegetable market and Angol.

More recently wheat and cattle have faced competition in liquid form. Chilean wine has gained a good reputation on the international scene establishing new export markets with the result that new wine regions have been developed and viticulture has expanded. A visit to the Valle de Colchagua between San Fernando and Pichilemu confirms that the wineries are run by very wealthy families; the vineyards spread out around attractive haciendas bearing witness to the magnificence of past times. Some have even become well known as museums.

A lively scene at the fish market of Valparaíso (far left, top). – In the morning, when the fishermen return with their catch, the fish are sold directly from the boats at the Caleta Portales between Valparaíso and Viña del Mar (above). – Fishing is not everything; sometimes you just need time to read the newspaper (bottom left).

A South-Seas Paradise: Anakena Beach on Easter Island with the seven moai.

Robinson and the Center of the Universe

Easter Island and the Juan Fernández Archipelago

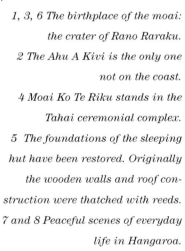

1, 3, 6 The birthplace of the moai: the crater of Rano Raraku.
2 The Ahu A Kivi is the only one not on the coast.
4 Moai Ko Te Riku stands in the Tahai ceremonial complex.
5 The foundations of the sleeping hut have been restored. Originally the wooden walls and roof construction were thatched with reeds.
7 and 8 Peaceful scenes of everyday life in Hangaroa.

2

4

For its inhabitants it is the center of the universe; for everyone else, it is the remotest place on earth: Easter Island is known to the Spanish as Isla de Pascua and to its inhabitants as Rapa Nui. It was discovered on Easter Sunday 1722 by Jakob Roggeveen, the captain of a Dutch trading ship. And so he dubbed the island.

Rapa Nui, the Center of the Universe. From their point of view, the inhabitants are quite right. The island is surrounded by ocean on all sides; nothing interrupts the monotony. Chile is 3,700 kilometers (2,313 miles) away. The inhabitants of Easter Island arrived from Polynesia in about 400 B.C, having sailed thousands of miles in boats.

5

6

The sea plays an important role in their mythology.

Easter Island is celebrated for its giant stone statues, the moai. They stand lined up in groups around the coast, staring out to sea through eyes of corals and shells; only one group gazes inland. When the first Europeans landed on Easter Island, one of whom was a certain Georg Forster from Mainz, they found confusion: many of the volcanic rock statues had fallen over or were broken. The foreign visitors speculated that the under-privileged "Short Ears" had re-belled against the ruling "Long Ears" caste.

Colonial rulers can never be accused of treating indigenous cultures with great dignity or mas-sive interest, and so much of the real narrative is veiled with un-certainty. It is only 60 years or so since that the island inhabi-tants were actually liberated from their ghetto-like existence. From that time the Rapa Nui have adhered to their own cultural tra-ditions.

The inhabitants of the Juan Fer-nández archipelago did not have these problems; they were origi-nally crayfish fishermen and lob-ster-catchers who settled on the islands from Chile. Aside from their unique birdlife, the dense forests characteristic of volcanic islands and quality of the lobsters, the Islas Juan Fernández have one further point of veritable interest for it here that Robinson Crusoe, alias Alexander Selkirk, was marooned, providing Daniel Defoe with inspiration for one of the best-known stories of world literature. The "real" Selkirk had been aboard the trading ship "Cinque Ports" in 1704 and had quarrelled so violently with the captain that he asked to be put ashore. The islands are now known as Robinson Crusoe and Alexander Selkirk.

Huasos, Gold Mines and Esoterics

The Norte Chico

Springtime comes to the
Valle Hurtado: blossoming cactuses
in the Cordillera (below).

Journey's end at the hacienda
(above). – Two huasos on a trip
through a grove of blossoming
almond trees (right-hand page).

Last year, the wealthy Don Casanova suffered a crushing defeat at the hands of a German waitress named Christine. The occasion was the annual rodeo in Chañar, a tiny hamlet of 318 inhabitants in the valley of the Río Hurtado. Christine had attracted attention in the trials for the horse races, but in fact she should not really have been allowed to start because she did not own a race horse. But Don Casanova, who became obsessed by the idea of competing against Christine, demonstrated his generosity by lending her one. When, however, he arrived to take part in the contest wearing the woolen poncho and the broad-brimmed hat of an honorable huas, all he saw of Christine was the flowing hair and the thundering hooves of his horse.

This year he is back again to uphold the traditions in style. He laughs a little ruefully when he speaks of his defeat by Christine.

Only aficionados like Don Casanova have no problem finding the way to Chañar, which is no more than a tiny dot on the map. The road from Ovalle to Samo Alto is asphalt, but the road after is no more than a winding gravel track. Here the Río Hurtado has carved its bed between dusty mountainsides which rise up more than 4,800 meters (15,748 feet). Flowing from the Andes towards Ovalle, its banks are carpeted with a luxuriant green. Exceptionally fertile agricultural land on which fields of fruit and vegetables thrive marks the river's course.

When a rodeo takes place Chañar is transformed into the secret capital of the Norte Chico. Throughout the region, poplar

The Plaza de Armas of the former mining town of Copiapó radiates a hint of the atmosphere of the 19th-century period of expansion (above and below). – Dominated by the landmark lighthouse, the sandy beach of La Serena extends for miles (center).

trees have been planted in great number to protect the village from the harsh winds. The semi-desert region's vegetation contains many various species of cactus so many in fact that they are too numerous for dictionaries to translate their names. Here is the center of the cattle-breeding region. The hordes of visitors cast a critical eye on the contests, which range from the herding of cattle to the horse-taming. In the evening there are tasting sessions for pisco, the national schnapps produced from a local grape.

If you go hiking in the mountains you will soon arrive in gold-digger country. In the valley below everything flourishes in the little river oases: peaches, avocados, dates, plums, mirabelles, water melons, grapes. At high altitude, beneath the scrubby vegetation, veins of metal run beneath the bare rocks.

Gold in the Mountains

Even in the days of the Inca, gold was mined here. For the Incas, gold was sacred and was used for making ceremonial objects. Even before the Incas, the Diaguita had found gold. The tribe, known for beautifully painted pottery – some claim the finest in all of South America – stemmed from what is now Argentina, was colonized by the Incas. The entrance to an abandoned goldmine is easy to access from Chañar, but there is little to see save a narrow black opening in the rock wall which the workers had to squeeze past.

It is just one of many thousands in a region the conquistadors praised to the heavens. Those gold seekers had the idea that the more inhospitable the mountain, the more valuable the metal concealed in its depths. The judgement of the Spanish conquerors was basically correct. But here in the desolate far north of Chile, it was not quite as easy as the gold in the Inca kingdom of the two priest-kings Atahualpa and Huáscar in Peru. There it had already been mined and worked and all that was required was to gather it up and load their ships. Here it had to be mined – a task obviously far too arduous for the foreign invaders.

Charles Darwin travelled through North Chile in 1833 and noted in his "Voyage of the Beagle" diary, somewhat disparagingly, that the region looked like an anthill – a result of the exca-

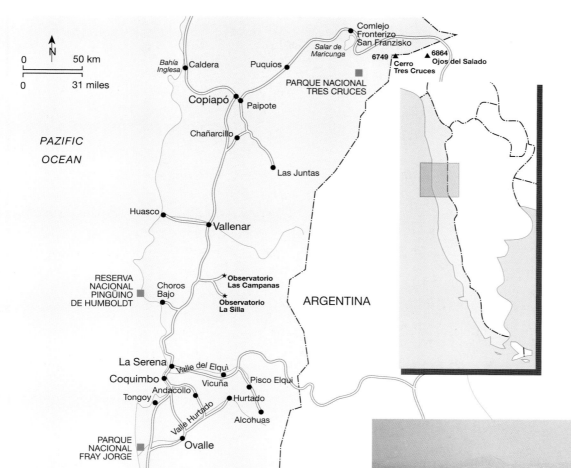

vation of countless mines. In less than 300 years, much had occurred.

After the Wars of Independence the Spanish had been expelled from the land, and the Chilean government surveyed and explored the country. The scientists' discoveries confirmed the conquistadors' veracity regarding inhospitable mountains and richer discoveries of gold.

Veins of copper, gold and silver ran beneath the scrub vegetation, and the Chileans appropriated what the colonial rulers had disdainfully ignored. In a period of approximately 60 years the land, vegetation and living conditions were investigated; during this time the most important mining discoveries were made; the most significant being almost symbolic in character. In 1832, in Chañarcillo, a vein was discovered which turned out to be the third-largest silver deposit in the world. The revenues from this mine alone enabled the country to repay all its overseas debts.

The erosion landscapes behind the coast of the Pan de Azúcar National Park extend for miles (center). – A young couple on the Pacific Coast near Caldera (below).

63

Intensive irrigation is possible in the valleys. The dry, sunny climate even encourages palm trees to grow – as well as grapes, fruit and vegetables. The broad slopes beneath the snow-capped peaks of the Cordillera are paradise for those who want to follow the cowboy trail (above and bottom left). – This thorny plant is popularly known as "mother-in-law's chair" (far right).

64

These glittering highlights may have been exhausted, but the mineral deposits of the Norte Chico have lost nothing of their economic significance: the mining of barium sulphate, copper, iron, marble and gold is the most significant source of employment in the region to this day.

Not far from Samo Alto and Chañar beside the Río Hurtado is the little mining town of Andacollo. Slag heaps and mountains, whose forests provided fuel for the smelting furnaces, surround a narrow valley which has just enough space for a village. Other veins may be spent, but mining continues here. Around Christmas time thousands of pilgrims journey from the highlands to the Church of Our Lady of the Rosary in Andacollo. The little wooden Madonna is the patron saint of miners; she comes from Lima and is said to have appeared to miners who were buried underground.

Railways into Isolation

One of the greatest challenges for Chile, a thinly populated land with long distances between villages and towns, was the settling

Only bold travelers come here in winter: the grandiose panorama of the Laguna Santa Rosa with the Ojos del Salado on the horizon looks enchanted and unreal under a layer of snow and ice. The journey is quite an adventure at this time of year. Unexpected snowstorms and vientos blancos far from human habitation at an altitude of 4,000 meters (13,123 feet) are just some of the hazards (all photos).

of the countryside and the establishment of links between the settlements. The government was successful in the Norte Chico. Like the British, who were later involved in the mining industry, they had to find a means of transporting the goods. Railway lines soon criss-crossed the region, but only where they were viable – in other words, from the mines to the Pacific ports. The first line between Copiapó and Caldera was completed in 1850; the last, between Vallenar and Huasco, was constructed by the North Americans in 1892. The boom is long over now and the old stations have been turned into museums.

The regions were settled according to their economic viability. Accommodation was built for the workers and a minimum of infrastructure followed, so that in some cases the worker's families could live there too. It was of no consequence that the immediate environment was often hostile and that neither water nor fuel was available. The settlements were abandoned when the mines were closed down.

This can be clearly seen east of Copiapó, on the route between Paipote and Puquios. The railway was abandoned long

66

ago. It is dusty and hot, and at night temperatures sink below freezing point.

Puquios was abandoned in 1930. A single farmhouse along the route is still inhabited; the farmer and his wife make a living raising goats and selling the cheese. Don Francisco calls himself "Sherpa" and scanning his sunburnt face it is impossible to guess how old he might be. He once worked for the mining company as a scout. Knowing the region well he could give advance warning of the notorious "white winds", the *vientos blancos* – sudden and frequent snowstorms which cause people to lose orientation completely.

We press on through this lonely region towards the Tres Cruces National Park and arrive at the Laguna del Negro Francisco and Laguna Rosa. Both lie on the border with Argentina. The Ojos del Salado, the highest volcano in the world (6,880 meters/22,572 feet) is Chile's highest mountain. Steeped in unusual colors, it stands like a sentinel over an unreal landscape. The mountains glow in shades of warm chocolate brown, aubergine and apricot. Flamingoes stalk along the lake shores and the lagoons, their surfaces strewn with a fine layer of salt, sparkling deep blue or orange and red. Salt is mined here – and gold. The Marte mine is at a staggering 5,000 meters altitude (16,404 feet).

Unlike the bad old days, miners now work regular hours for good wages and paid holidays. They work eight days straight followed by eight days off. All those setting out for the Laguna Verde, the starting point for climbing the Ojos del Salado, is registered at the beginning of the mining region – and is happy to know he will not be forgotten in the midst of all this solitude.

In the Land of the Dinosaurs

The biological research station at the Laguna del Negro Francisco discovered dinosaurs had lived in these icy altitudes. The discovery of bones and fossils indicate this region, now so desolate and bare, must once have been thick with dense vegetation. Nowadays, in the face of so much rock, scree and sand it is barely imaginable.

See page 73

Focusing on the Southern Cross

Observatories in the Desert

1 The 15-meter (49-foot) ESO Sweden telescope in the La Silla Observatory. – 2 Telescopes in the observatory at El Paranal, to the south of Antofagasta. – 3 In the control room at La Silla Observatory. During the early evening the telescopes at La Silla are prepared for the next session. The octagonal structure contains the 3.6 meter (12-foot) high-resolution telescope (NTT). – 4 The large parabolic reflecting telescopes of the ESO Observatory at La Silla lie beyond the coastal mists to the north of La Serena. – 5 The optical unit of the great NTT telescope at La Silla.

Of all the mysteries scientists investigate, the study of the universe is probably the one which most captures the public imagination. A mythical element is involved. Who does not like to star-gaze at night, counting comets' tails, studying meteorites in museums, observing lunar eclipses at night and waiting for Halley's Comet? A single glimpse of the heavens is sufficient for us to ponder the unsolved mysteries of the universe, which have fascinated mankind for thousands of years.

Planetariums and observatories are extremely popular. But no matter where in the world you may be, only a vital combination of favorable conditions will permit an un-

obstructed view of the firmament. Sparsely populated North Chile has precisely these qualities; far enough from cities causing light pollution and industrial smog, possessing greatly arid deserts, high peaks and a high frequency of nights which are atmospherically

crystal clear. Driving through the Valle del Elqui you can glimpse the white ellipses of El Tololo Observatory perched on a mountain ridge, and La Silla, the European Southern Observatory (ESO), nearby. In El Paranal, two hours' drive from Antofagasta, the ESO

68

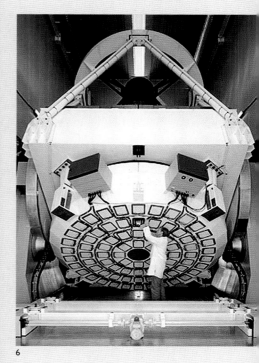

6

5

has installed the VLT, the Very Large Telescope, a linked system of four telescopes each 8.2 meters (26.9 feet) in diameter and all at the cutting edge of the latest scientific technology.

Perched on a mountain ridge at an altitude of 2,400 meters (7,874 feet), La Silla in the Norte Chico, was constructed in 1969 as an ESO project involving ten European countries. It has excellent telescopes for the exploration of space. The New Technology Telescope, installed in 1989, was something of a sensation at the time, consisting of a thin, lightweight ceramic plate on 75 adjustable supports all of which enable it to be moved electronically into the ideal

position. The mirror is 3.5 meters (11.5 feet) in diameter. The latest acquisition in La Silla is SEST, the enormous Swedish-ESO Submillimetre Telescope; it is 15 meters (49 feet) in diameter and capable of measurements precise to just a single millimeter.

La Silla, El Paranal and El Tololo, supported by a number of universities from the entire American continent, are not the only observatories in the north of the country. The USA operates a site in Las Campanas.

La Silla, El Tololo and Las Campanas are not open to the public. El Paranal can be visited on selected weekends during the daytime. Be warned, it is such an attraction you

should book your visit several months in advance.

The Observatorio Comunal Mamalluca near Vicuña in the Valle del Elqui is, by contrast, a popular institution permitting the interested amateur to explore the heavens. Lectures are held at night, and visitors can observe the skies through a 30-centimeter (12-inch) telescope.

The first European astronomers were totally confused by the southern skies. The heavens of the northern and southern hemispheres are completely different in appearance. Visitors to Mamalluca can see this clearly. One constellation which everyone seeks to identify is the "Southern Cross", once a vital navigational aid for thousands of seafarers.

Rare species of cactus flourish in the Pan de Azúcar National Park.

Let us put our imagination to use again. Here, where today's aspiring mountaineers warm their frozen limbs in the hot springs of the Laguna Verde, on their way to the peak of the Ojos del Salado, is a mountain pass. Until the 1960s, North Argentinean cattle farmers drove their herds across from the Argentinean pampas to Chilean seaports for they were nearer than the Argentinean Atlantic ports. It is only 80 kilometers (50 miles) from the peaks of the Andes to the Pacific.

Climbing up to these lofty heights of around 4,600 meters (15,092 feet) yourself, you immediately realize how exhausting it must have been. Mountaineers planning to climb the Ojos del Salado sleeping overnight in refuges run by the Chilean Department of the Environment and Forestry are required beforehand to spend about a week acclimatizing.

In the Valley of Pisco

The Norte Chico does not consist only of solitude and the grandiose former habitats of dinosaurs,

abandoned railway lines, dried-out salt lagoons and snow-capped mountain peaks.

Pisco grapes are grown in the Elqui Valley. The region is covered with *parronales*, horizontal spaliers, tracing impressively long or short shadows as the earth takes its course around the sun. Pisco has been distilled here in large quantities since the early 20th century. In those days the various distilleries were scattered across the valley, like "Los Artesanos" in Monte Grande or "RR" in Pisco Elqui. Today "Pisco Capel" is the market leader. You can visit the distillery and taste its wares.

The Valle del Elqui is famous for more than just schnapps. It is also a hippie paradise: remote, peaceful, exceptionally attractive – and remarkably difficult to live in. The hippie communes have selected the most inaccessible villages close to the Argentine border as their new home. Cochiguaz and Alcoguas are still not easy to reach.

There is no doubt that the region has a magical atmosphere. The clear, pure air and the dramatic mountain peaks rising behind the deeply cut river valley make an unusual setting. Those with a propensity for the esoteric saw in them a great likeness to the Himalayas claiming to sense similar fields of energy.

However you may regard such theories, courses in meditation and relaxation, treatment with healing plants and Gestalt therapy are just some of the not unpleasant side-effects the Valle del Elqui has gained since being developed as an esoteric center.

Amongst the beauties of the Norte Chico, La Serena enchants visitors with its harmonious colonial architecture (left-hand page). The unusually luxuriant vegetation along the course of the river in the Elqui Valley contrasts with the inhospitable, desert-like mountains of the Cordillera. It is ideal for the cultivation of the pisco grape (above). – A quaint newspaper kiosk in the coastal

You can stay the night in the "Alma Zen" or in the "Sol Naciente".

They belong together like patchouli perfume oil and joss sticks: the Buddhist art gallery with DVD messages from the guru and the shop selling soap perfumed with flowers; the home-made planetarium in the garden and UFOs in the dead of the night. Some enchanted ideas can even be turned into ready cash, but perhaps we would be wiser just to invest in a bottle of pisco.

Gabriela Mistral, one of the most important lyric poets of the 20th century, grew up in the untamed beauty of this landscape. The Nobel Prize for Literature is usually awarded to male writers

Rugged black rocks along the coast in the Pan de Azúcar National Park (below). The pelicans on the rocks have been busy: the guano, bird droppings was once a highly prized fertilizer exported as far as Europe (right-hand page, top). – Below can be seen the various species of wildlife of the Isla Damas, protected by the National Park and accessible from Punta Chorros (all photos).

and only few women have garnered this high award. One, however, is the Chilean teacher from the Elqui Valley, Lucila Godoy Alcayaga. She was awarded the prize in 1945. Her memory is preserved by monuments and museums in Vicuña and Monte Grande.

La Serena

Let us follow the curving road from the Valle del Elqui to La Serena, the capital of the Norte Chico. For many years the town has been divided into two sections: the old town center and the new resort area bordering the long sandy beach. Hotels, apartment blocks, restaurants, taverns and shopping arcades form an independent center, extremely popular during the mild summers.

La Serena was originally founded in 1544 by the Spanish conquistadors. It was planned as a re-provisioning port for the line of bases established southwards along the coast, beginning in Peru. In 1544 approximately 800 Indian slaves and 100 whites lived there. La Serena is one of the oldest colonial cities on the continent, although nothing remains from those early years. The architecture is remarkably harmonious. The public buildings around the Plaza de Armas, one of the most attractive in the entire country, are all in a robust colonial style and painted in off-white and brick red. Their attractive appearance was the work of one of the town's most famous sons, Gabriel González Videla, who became the President of Chile during the late 1940s and who subsequently channelled funds into the renovation of his native town.

A rough, wild landscape: the coast near Chañaral.

The White Gold of the North

Nitrates, Chile's First Major Export

1 Pictures from past times: When nitrates were found and subsequently mined between the twin ranges of the Cordillera in northern Chile, the sun-scorched empty high plains suddenly came to life. Little remains of the towns today.

1 A graveyard recalls those who died. – 2 Wall paintings along the Avenida Baquedano in the port of Iquique recall times past. Photos of the restored nitrates oficina at Humberstone: the Esplanade (3) and the theater (4) as well as remains of old machines (5). – 6 The Oficina Laura, one of the partially restored mining complexes, lies opposite Humberstone.

In 1789, the year of the French Revolution, a young botanist from Bohemia set out for South America. On his exploratory journeys through Peru, Bolivia and Chile, Thaddäus Haenke found something which, within a hundred years, would lead to a declaration of war and the re-drawing of the map of southern South America. His discovery had been nitrate deposits.

Haenke came across them more or less halfway between Iquique and Antofagasta, on the high plains which extend behind the coastal mountain ranges. Tarapacá und Antofagasta, the two most northerly regions of Chile were at that time within the borders of Peru and Bolivia.

Tamarugal, a plant with an extensive root system, flourishes in the salt-rich soil of the Norte Grande and produces nitrate, as do the cactuses growing in that region. Nitrate deposits are found on rocks and stones as a result of decomposition. Being available on the surface, extraction was an easy task.

In 1809, Thaddäus Haenke developed a method for crystallizing *caliche*, nitrate salts, from raw nitrate. He found it equally easy to determine the characteristics of nitrate and that it could be used as an effective fertilizer. As industrialisation took hold in Europe it met with huge demand.

Seven or eight nitrate factories were founded in the region around

Tarapacá between 1810 and 1812. From the mid-1830s the valuable substance was exported and sold to Europe and the United States. Trade with the Old World made the industry prosper.

In 1866, Chilean Santos Ossa discovered nitrate in what was formerly Bolivia and started production in the "Salar del Carmen." By this time Chileans, British, Germans and French had all become involved in the Bolivian-Peruvian industry.

In 1879 Chile declared war on Peru and Bolivia, when the latter two countries broke a previous agreement and levied export taxes. Four years later, with Britain's support, (the colonial power's share of interest in the nitrate business was

all that is left of some is just a few broken down walls. Were it not for the countless graveyards where the nitrates workers were given their most final rest, it would be hard to guess what these heaps of stones represent.

The museums of Antofagasta and Iquique provide ample information for visitors interested in finding out more about the nitrates industry. You can also see at first hand what the factories used to look like in the restored Oficinas Humberstone (on the outskirts of Iquique) and Chacabuco (halfway between Antofagasta and Calama). Augusto Pinochet used Chacabuco as a prison camp during his military dictatorship. On the initiative of the Goethe Institute it has been restored as a memorial to recent history.

3

4

virtually 60 percent) Chile was victorious. Tarapacá and Antofagasta were ceded to Chile, guaranteeing control over all the nitrate deposits.

A few years on and nitrates gained even greater interest as an export, for they could also be used in the production of gunpowder and in 1914 Europe staged World War I.

Today the high plains are almost entirely uninhabited and it is hard to believe that almost 100,000 men once lived and worked here. The camps are marked on old maps but

In the Home of the Mapuche

The Norte Grande

Particularly in the early morning, the Tatio geysers provide tourists with a spectacular display (center).

You can enjoy a refreshing swim in the Baños de Puritama (below). – Survivors in the icy climate: rock-hard lichens at an altitude of 4,400 meters (14,436 feet) on Parinacota Volcano in Lauca National Park (right).

At the crack of dawn, hiking boots covered in reddish sand, hair standing on end, noses sunburnt and heads cold and dull, we left San Pedro de Atacama, on the edge of the driest desert in the world. The newly risen sun, shedding its first rays, began to warm us. A handful of dogs, heads hanging, lolled across the little square dotted with pepper trees. All others were still asleep in the low adobe houses. There was no sign of breakfast anywhere. We unpacked the cookies and oranges, and of course, our water bottles.

A baseball cap and water bottle are the distinguishing marks of the holidaymaker in San Pedro. The sun shines mercilessly on the top of your head, and the desert makes you thirsty. You ask yourself how the inhabitants of San Pedro managed to survive without baseball caps and water bottles before the tourists arrived.

Quite well, in fact. For no Atacameño would ever have dreamt of riding 30 kilometers (19 miles) on a mountain bike in order to find Indian burial grounds, or walking to the *ayllus*, unless he had good reason to visit the village communities surrounding San Pedro. In the searing heat of the day the Atacameños retreat to the cool interior of their houses made of clay bricks, which have been built that way for centuries, meaning it is almost impossible to tell the difference between old and the new houses. They would never think of climbing Licancabur Volcano, which rises almost 6,000 meters (19,685 feet) and can be seen from the village, majestically looming over the dry and dusty landscape around it. Even in their wildest dreams, the inhabitants

of San Pedro would never imagine getting up at 4 a.m. to walk through darkness to visit the Tatio geysers.

Moonlight above the Valley

San Pedro de Atacama is approximately 100 kilometers (63 miles) southeast of the Chuquicamata, it is the world's largest surface copper mine, surrounded by a ring of canals of bubbling water. It looks almost archaic, a landscape of salt pans glinting in the sunlight around which flamingos search for food, rusty colored mighty volcanoes, placid green lagoons with white salty rims and an eerie lunar like valley where erosion, wind, blistering

The Indian settlements of the Norte Grande lie scattered between the lofty summits and the high plains. A snapshot from Caspana: a farmer with his donkeys and a farmer's wife feeding the goats (above and right). – The port of Antofagasta's most famous landmark is La Portada, a limestone arch standing in the sea (center).

sun and freezing night temperatures have formed a bizarre vocabulary of unreal shapes.

San Pedro de Atacama and its surroundings are enchanting. Unfortunately they have to come to terms with both the positive and negative aspects of development. The trappings of tourism (hotels, pubs, bars, travel agents en masse) appear a mixed blessing. They are changing the little town's unique atmosphere. Whilst enabling visitors to sleep and eat here and to enjoy the beauty of the desert the downside is that with it prostitution and drugs have come to a village in which only 15 years ago its main contact with the outside world consisted of the arrival on Tuesdays of a VW van with fresh bread and cakes from the nearest town.

To be in San Pedro is akin to stepping out of the everyday world. 2,500 meters (8,200 feet) above sea level, home of the nation's foremost anthropological museum and springboard for excursions to see natural wonders at altitudes above

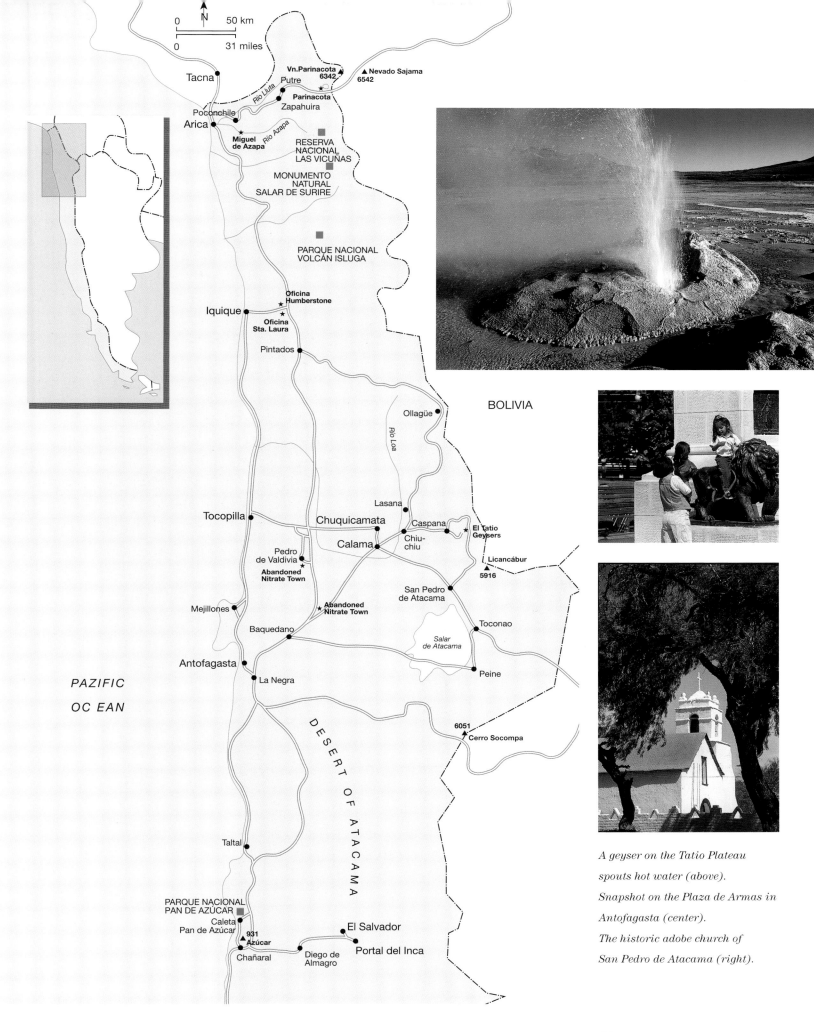

N

0   50 km

0   31 miles

Tacna

Vn.Parinacota
6342
▲ Nevado Sajama
6542

Putre

Parinacota

Zapahuira

Poconchile

Arica

Río Lluta

Río Azapa

Miguel
de Azapa

RESERVA
NACIONAL
LAS VICUÑAS

MONUMENTO
NATURAL
SALAR DE SURIRE

PARQUE NACIONAL
VOLCÁN ISLUGA

Oficina
Humberstone

Iquique

Oficina
Sta. Laura

Pintados

BOLIVIA

Ollagüe

Río Loa

Lasana

Caspana

El Tatio
Geysers

Tocopilla

Chuquicamata

Chiu-
chiu

Calama

Licancábur
5916

Pedro
de Valdivia

Abandoned
Nitrate Town

San Pedro
de Atacama

Mejillones

Abandoned
Nitrate Town

Toconao

Baquedano

Salar
de Atacama

Antofagasta

Peine

La Negra

PAZIFIC

OC EAN

6051
Cerro Socompa

DESERT OF ATACAMA

Taltal

PARQUE NACIONAL
PAN DE AZÚCAR

Caleta
Pan de Azúcar

931
Azúcar

El Salvador

Portal del Inca

Chañaral

Diego de
Almagro

A geyser on the Tatio Plateau
spouts hot water (above).
Snapshot on the Plaza de Armas in
Antofagasta (center).
The historic adobe church of
San Pedro de Atacama (right).

5,000 meters (16,400 feet). San Pedro is one of Chile's main attractions, not only for its solitary beauty but also because it seems to be a place beyond ordinary time.

The Open Sky

There was the legacy of antiquity, which in spite of its international appeal and the ring money through the tourist companies' tills, was ignored at first by the Chileans. And there was their national pride, which also guaranteed jobs, training and good pay at the Chuquicamata. What did the "open sky", *cielo abierto*, as the locals dubbed the copper mine, look like before the Guggenheim brothers took over its exploitation in 1910? One dome more in the seemingly endless succession tucked away in the Andean Cordillera? Since then, five percent of the world's copper supplies have been extracted from the mine whose name tells of the region's Aymara heritage. In 2002, 1,300,000 tonnes of copper, and other ores such as sulfide, selenium and molybdenum, were dug out from here.

The metal plant within the state-owned mine stinks, hisses and puffs smoke into the sky. The latter gleams in shades of

The Laguna Chaxa in the Salar de Atacama glints in the golden light cast by the last rays of the evening sun (top). Chilean flamingos hunt for food in the saline waters (above).

84

green and reddish clouds. For almost a decade the Codelco Company has tried to reduce the long-term damage to the environment. It is, of course, incalculable. The contracts drawn up for the Chuquicamata are of limited duration; the medical care they and their families receive is more intensive than the norm.

Those who prefer not to reside at 3,000 meters (9,842 feet) can settle instead in Calama. The little town lies at a lower altitude and was planned as a dormitory town, but that is a label it does not accept for itself. The most expensive hotel rooms are to be found here and eating is not exactly cheap, either. On Wednesdays backpackers kill time in the lovely shady square before their train leaves for the Bolivian capital, La Paz.

A Leap Back in Time

From bustling Calama you can embark on a journey back in time. Traveling toward Bolivia, you will come across pre-Inca fortifications set in a landscape of geysers and largely extinct volcanoes. Protected by rocks and natural embankments, they were built at the end of deep canyons. The most important and best-preserved (and restored) is the Pukara Lasana in the Río Loa valley. Before

you reach the towering complex, which once had a roof of algarrobo wood, you will pass a number of isolated Indian farmsteads. The Aymara grow carrots, leeks and potatoes in the damp valley soil. The Pukara Lasana dates from the 12th century and has a 110 buildings in all. The Pukara at Turi must have been even larger; it was built of volcanic rock by the Atacameños. The Inca, who colonized the Atacameños, also used it before they themselves were driven out by the Spanish conquistadors.

Visitors interested in the pukaras will discover villages like Aiquina on their occasionally difficult journey. Gonzalo, our guide, told us of his aunt and her house, which he insisted we should see. En route we passed the deep gorge of the Salado, the Cuenca del Diablo; in earlier times it had to be crossed in a sort of cable-car.

Gonzalo's aunt's house was small, dark and empty apart from a few tufts of grass forcing their way through the cracks in the floor. Most of the houses in Aiquina look like this one and are usually only intended for guests attending the Festival of the Virgin of Guadalupe in Aiquina. The rest of the year they remain vacant until the pilgrimage begins on September 7. Tens of thousands of pilgrims stream to this remote place, which normally has a population of only 50 inhabitants. They come to ask the Virgin to intercede for them or to thank her for the fulfillment of a request. It is a colorful festival with shared rituals and a dance by dervishes.

It is hard to imagine that the 400 inhabitants of the yet more remote and ancient village of Caspana grow the flowers which are sold at the Feria Modelo in Calama. It is a difficult journey for the traders. But not only do the inhabitants of Caspana manage to bring their flowers to market, they have also created a fine museum 3,300 meters (10,827 feet)above sea level and far away from the rest of the world. It provides information about customs and tradition, this recording of local history is also a means of sustaining their identity.

The Fascination of Nitrate

Our journeys through the north of Chile introduced us to impressive natural phenomena and much solitude. It seems incredible that this region, dominated by deserts featuring vast stretches of land where time seems to have stood still, was once full of life and produced Chile's first major export: nitrate (see page 78).

In those days, nitrates were as valuable as gold, since they served as the basis for fertilizers. The demand was great on its own shores but even more so in Central Europe. The nitrates were deposited like a white, furry coating on the rocks of the empty high plains. They were produced naturally by the decomposition of cactuses which were dried by the sunny desert air. The entire region parallel to the coast was full of them.

This wealth lured traders, merchants, speculators and soldiers of fortune. They came from England, Germany and Chile and they soon shared out the business between themselves. The fishermen, who caught and tenderized squid along the black rocky coast, did not share in this prosperity.

The nitrates required a port for their shipping abroad. Initially Iquique was chosen, a Cinderella of a village like the other impoverished fishermen's settlements in the region. It marked the beginning of a new chapter. Countless items were needed for the pioneer settlement: building materials, fabrics, furniture, china, wood, pipes, machines, wire and especially water. Engineers and workers arrived. Trading companies were established and passenger jetties constructed. All the experts and nitrates barons who settled there wanted a social stage where they could see and be seen. The distractions of big cities – balls, concert, dinners – had to be made available in Iquique.

No sooner said than done. Wooden villas in Louisiana style appeared along the Avenida Baquedano, which became the town promenade. The square acquired benches and a snow-white belfry. One of the first opera houses on the sub-continent was built, seven years before the famous one in Manaus in Brazil which

See page 92

A big festival for a little Virgin: together with thousands of pilgrims, dancers from Northern Chile and musicians from Bolivia celebrate the Festival of the Virgin Mary of Aiquina on the edge of the Atacama Desert (all photos).

Bastions against the Invaders

The Indian Pukaras

1 People often resort to tales of extra-terrestrials to explain a phenomenon like this geoglyph in the desert sands: the Gigante de Atacama is 86 m (282 ft) tall.
2 One of the most imposing Indian fortresses is the Pukara de Lasana, which lies above a river oasis.
3 The dry desert climate has preserved Indian mummies, like this exhibit in the Museum of San Pedro de Atacama, extremely well.
4 The old Indian town of Tulor Viejo – shown here are the reconstructions of some of the buildings – dates from the 5–8th centuries B.C.

The Spanish wiped out the history of the original inhabitants of South America. They regarded the Indian tribes as inferior, coercing them into forced labor and persuading them to give up their religion, traditions and culture. Their places of worship and their homes were destroyed. The arrival of the Spanish in Chile and elsewhere became the beginning of historical records. Indian peoples such as the Atacameños had no written language which would have enabled them to pass on their culture to future generations.

The Archaeology departments of the universities of Northern Chile in Antofagasta and Arica have excavated a settlement at Tulor, south of San Pedro de Atacama from the desert sand. They have revealed circular, linked remains of walls dating from the 8th century B.C. The original appearance of the buildings has been reconstructed and they feature round, windowless houses with low arched doorways.

Near San Pedro is a pukara, or fortress, attributed to the Atacameños proving that the region was continuously inhabited. Built in the 12th century, the pukara at Quitor clings to the hillside while appearing to cascade down the mountainside into the Río Pedro valley. The houses were built of stone, with clay replacing the mortar.

The best example of a pukara is the one at Lasana, which is more grandiose and in a better state of repair. It is easily reached from Calama via a scenic excursion through the picturesque village of Chiu Chiu.

The Río Loa has carved out a deep bed framed on either side by steeply rising mountainsides. On

88

4

the left-hand side, at an altitude of 2,500 meters (8,200 feet), at the point where the road seems to peter out, towers the massive, pale gray Pukara de Lasana, an imposing complex once consisting of 110 buildings. The roofs, made of algarrobo wood, have not survived. As you clamber around you can see that Lasana was obviously built like a village. Cobbled alleys lead past the houses and storage buildings. Lasana dates from the 12th century.

The most impressive complex of all lies further towards Bolivia. The Pukara de Turi was also built during the 12th century and was extended and used as a fortress by the Inca. It dominates a high plateau 3,100 meters (10,170 feet) above sea level and demonstrates the same architectural urban layout as Lasana with squares, alleys and houses built of volcanic rock located at right angles to each other.

If you set out from Arica to visit Lauca National Park, you will pass the fortifications at Copaiquilla.

Tarapacá University in Arica is supervising the reconstruction of around 400 houses overlooking a deep canyon. The slope was previously terraced, to increase the area of cultivable land.

Nearby, but scattered across the mountains and deep valleys and therefore inaccessible unfortunately are the pukaras of Belén, Lupica and Chapiquiña. This makes it quite clear how densely populated and accessible the region was even during the 12th century.

The spread of Chapiquiña is at an altitude of 3,200 meters (10,500 feet). San Miguel de Azapa University has excavated two of the attached burial grounds.

Below the Lascar Volcano near Toconao.

drove Werner Herzog's "Fitzcarraldo" to distraction. Diagonally opposite, in the "Centro Español", interior decorators celebrated an orgy of Moorish-Andalusian decorative style. It is worth seeing to this day, and the food there is excellent.

The bays and headlands of the north coast experienced a boom – only for those who could afford it, of course. For the workers who toiled in the nitrate extraction plants, the attractions of Iquique were not available. They lived in barracks near the plants, and their wages were paid in fake metal currency which the factory itself produced. They could use it to purchase goods in the factory store – at inflated prices. Schnapps was cheaper than drinking water.

92

Nitrate made Iquique prosperous: old
wooden villas on the Avenida Baquedano
and a tram (left-hand page).
A bandstand and an attractive church
adorn the Plaza de Armas (below).

But then Iquique lost its supremacy as export harbor to Antofagasta. Today's capital of the Second Region looks like a working-class version of Iquique, despite its interesting 19th-century architecture and the ruins of Huanchaca, the former silver refinery, which was built in 1873 for the mines at Pulcayo and Oruro. The mighty stone walls provided a foundation for the processing machines.

The Panamericana between Antofagasta and Iquique is bordered by the ruins of long-abandoned nitrate extraction plants. A German chemist named Haber discovered how to produce synthetic fertilizer and the nitrates boom came to an abrupt end during the 1920s. Tens of thousands of men once worked here.

Of Flamingos and Miniature Camels

The little Andean camels and flamingos which live beside the salt pans are graceful and long-necked. The llama, alpaca, vicuña and guanaco are to the Indian cultures of South America what pig, horse, sheep and cattle are to those of Central Europe. They supply wool, meat and leather and are also used as beasts of burden. The vicuñas were almost made extinct for their precious wool, which is as light as a feather and has the same qualities as silk. A vicuña produces only 180 grams (6 ounces) every two years. The Aymara esteem the llama as a beast of burden with great stamina and prefer using alpaca for meat. The salt pans and lagoons of higher altitudes are the preferred habitat of the Andean flamingos, a threatened species. One of the most popular excursions from places like San Pedro de Atacam involves coming here to watch the animals at the salar. The flamingos feed on the algae and krill found beneath the salt layer in the lakes.

Today, the ruins stand alongside truck drivers' cafés with cheap plastic furniture and pinup calendars. And, of course, the graves. Graveyards were set up opposite the factories because there were no big towns in the vicinity. The graves are marked neither by stone monuments nor marble angels, but by brightly colored wooden crosses. Paper or plastic flowers provide non-fading decorations.

The North is Red

It was in the North that the first workers' uprisings took place. The trade unions were established here at an early date. The European immigrants working in the nitrates camps organized the first mine workers' strike in Iquique in 1907. It was put down by the army. "Whoever holds the North, holds Chile", was the watchword of Unidad Popular, the party of Salvador Allende, referring to the political might of the industrial workers of the region. They represented an influential political potential, and traditionally voted for the Left. Thus most of the yellowing photos showing Allende during the 1970 elections, were taken in the North.

Augusto Pinochet left his own bloody mark on the region by turning the nitrate Oficina Chacabuco, which had been closed down way back in 1939, into a concentration camp. It was the "Death Caravan of the North" and convinced public prosecutor Baltasar Garzón to have Pinochet arrested in 1999 and make the leader responsible for those actions.

From Sea Level to 4,600 Meters (15,000 feet)

Chile is made up of the twin chains of the Cordillera along with the central valley. In the far North, the mountains become fused together, with the highlands beginning immediately behind the coastal strip. The mountains rise so steeply behind the port of Arica that the region's favorite tourist excursion is also a doctor's nightmare, leading in less than eight hours from sea level up to 4,600 meters (15,000 feet) and then back again.

No visitor would want to miss the rapid changes of scenery, climbing from the gentle green valley oases of Lluta und Azapa up to the heights where the candelabra cacti grow. At the latest by the time you reach the village of Putre at 3,500 meters (11,483 feet) you should start chewing an extra coca leaf to avoid altitude sickness. The Aymara Indian Gerardo Pérez said that as an alter-

native an aspirin every hour would also combat the wobbly knees, headache and nauseous feeling in your stomach. He accompanied us up to the Parque Nacional Lauca and Lago Chungará. He enjoys outings like these: the sight of the vast, tranquil, emerald-green water framed by brightly striped volcanoes reaching a grand 6,000 meters (19,685 feet) is so beautiful it looks positively unreal.

Gerardo also proposed cultural excursions to see the life of the Indians in the Andes region. The Aymara, Atacameños, and Inca overlapped each other and also supplanted each other. Gerardo's journey takes him through Indian history: from Cusco in Peru, the epicenter of the Inca world, continuing across Lake Titicaca to see the Tihuanaco culture which once extended as far as San Pedro de Atacama, and to the pre-Incan Pukaras in Chile. The Indian aspects of Chile, naturally, do not stop at the Chilean border.

A view of the interior of the church of San Pedro de Atacama, with its cactus-wood roof (far left). Decorated with pink volcanic rock, the gleaming white adobe churches of the Altiplano all follow the same dualist principle: the belfry (the male principle) was built beside the church itself (the female principle). This can be clearly seen in Parinacota (above). Guallatire is tiny – not only when viewed from the belfry (left).

You may think you are dreaming – surreal landscapes: the Salar de Aguas Calientes on the way from San Pedro de Atacama to Argentina (right). – Flamingoes feed on microorganisms which live in the brackish water of the Salar de Surire (above).

In Valle de la Luna near San Pedro de Atacama.

Rails through the Desert

The railroads open up the country

1 A paradise (not only) for railroad fans: old steam engines "Made in Germany" in Baquedano Museum. – 2 There are countless tunnels along the routes through the Andes: The photo dates from around 1950. – 3 Supported by massive pillars, the railroad bridge crosses a valley near the Salto de Loja. – 4 An abandoned railroad station in the Atacama Desert west of Antofagasta. 5 Once the end of one of the most important railroad lines in South America, today looking rather museum-like: the station at Arica.

There were railroads in Chile long before the roads were built. From Antofagasta to Socompa; from Antofagasta to Mina Escondida and up to Iquique; from Arica to La Paz; from Calama to La Paz; from Copiapó to Caldera and Puquios; from Vallenar to Huasco; from Santiago to Puerto Montt; from Temuco to Maule and Freire – the rails criss-cross the land in a houndstooth check pattern.

Not all the routes make sense if one feels the prime function of railroads is to make traveling easier for people.

After all, who would want to travel from Copiapó into the wilderness of Puquios, where there is really nothing but desert and mountains and the occasional snowstorm? Chile's rail network was construct-

ed during the 19th century principally for the purposes of freight transport. The routes bear this fact out. It was built very early, in fact, and the route between Copiapó and the little port of Caldera was opened in 1850 to ship silver from Chañarcillo. The rail network soon linked the nitrate waste heaps and

warehouses in the Altiplano to the export harbors of Iquique and Antofagasta. Between the two towns and the oficinas, the stations are strung out like a row of beads.

In Antofagasta a freight train still clanks along the harbor, past the residential areas. It was originally

100

4

5

built by the Ferrocarriles Antofagasta-Bolivia (FCAB) company and is today a historic monument. Rails were laid from the gold and silver mines and the sulphur and lithium depots to Tocopilla and Chañaral, which fell into decline when the transports stopped. Today they continue to struggle bravely against the melancholy air which hangs over them. Sometimes the railroad workers left charming memorials behind, like the church tower built by the English at Caldera.

As far as tourists are concerned, two routes are of interest: from Santiago to Temuco and from Calama to La Paz. The train to Temuco has recently been restored and the railroad station in Santiago has always been an imposing construction of iron and steel.

Nostalgic travelers will be sad to learn of the demise of the old steam train manufactured by Linke-Hoffmann-Busch in Wroclaw in 1926, which once hauled the velvet-lined sleeping cars to Temuco in twelve hours.

And so, for lovers of adventurous railroad journeys, all that remains is the route from Calama to La Paz, which climbs to more than 4,000 meters (13,123 feet) across the Salar de Uyuni.

The journey takes 36 hours and on the Altiplano the temperatures sinks well below freezing.

The attractive stations remain; some of them, like those in Arica, Iquique, Antofagasta, Chacabuco, Caldera and Copiapó, have been classed as historic monuments. Some have even been turned into museums relating their histories. A railroad museum has already been opened in Baquedano.

Amongst the Indians and Germans

South of Santiago

A picture-postcard volcano: Osorno (above). – A family outing on Lago de Villarrica (below). – The best way to explore the forests and mountains of the South is on horseback (right-hand page).

Across the centuries, one of the rivers flowing through Southern Chile delineated the fictitious and actual boundary of so-called civilization. The Río Biobío flowing into the sea near the industrial city of Concepción, formed the southern boundary of the Spanish colony to the North. South of the river was Mapuche territory, the only Indian people the Spanish Conquista was unable to subjugate.

Southern Chile was a fiercely disputed region during the period of colonization. The Mapuche were unafraid of the white, bearded invaders and waged guerrilla warfare in defense of their fertile lands. Although they had never seen horses before they remained unafraid and undaunted by the sight of such alien quadrupeds. The moment they had a chance to defeat the Spanish and capture their weapons and horses, they did precisely that. And they made use of them too. Fernando, a Mapuche, told how horses were eaten at their banquets as a symbol of their national self-confidence.

Mexican Maya and Aztec myths, as well as Peruvian Inca legends claimed a white-skinned god would one day set foot in their country and compel the people to submit to him. These prophecies went a long way to explaining why the Spanish conquistadors were accepted as a foreign power. The Mapuche, on the other hand, had no such legends. For them the white men were simply enemies to be fought and defeated.

Pedro de Valdivia, the founder of Santiago, noted: "They fight like Germans", and continued to press ever further south, establishing settlements along the length of the country. But the

102

Mapuche revolted time and again and razed the enemy's dwellings to the ground in Angol, Concepción, Chillán, Osorno, Valdivia, Villarrica and La Imperial. The citizens were forced to flee through the territory of the Indians to seek refuge in Santiago.

When Pedro de Valdivia was killed fighting the Mapuche prince Lautaro, Pedro de Vizcarra, the Governor, went on to enslave all Indians and brand their faces. The Mapuche responded by forming an alliance with British pirates. Between 1545 and 1647, 42,000 Spanish soldiers were killed.

The Spanish failed to colonize the South during the colonial period. At first, missionaries attempted to establish churches south of the Biobío. A string of wars was followed by a succession of peace treaties. But no strategy succeeded in subduing the Mapuche. The last major uprising took place in 1655, after which the Mapuche were left in peace – for almost two hundred years.

Following independence in 1818 everything changed. The Chilean nation needed a country with fixed borders. Spanish colonial interests, however, had only focused on the exploitation of resources. They fought wherever there was something to be gained, sustaining heavy losses in the battles against the Mapuche. The Chileans, by contrast, had thousands of kilometers of borders to defend against the Argentinians,

Pictures of Cochamó:
A cooper at work (above) and the
shingle tower of the "Campo
Aventura", from here horse rides
set out into the dense forests of the
southern Lake District (right).
A row of brightly-painted wooden
houses in Villarrica, beside the
lake of the same name (center).

Bolivians and Peruvians and at the same time needed to consolidate the interior of the country. Rebellious Indian tribes were somewhat contrary to this scheme and made the country more vulnerable. Successive governments courted immigrants from Europe. The lands of the Mapuche would become appropriated, the people tricked by oppressive contracts and false promises, befuddled by alcohol they ended up being imprisoned in reservation-like areas.

The King of Patagonia

A French lawyer named Orllie-Antoine de Tounens got wind of what was happening. In 1856 he had come to love the noble

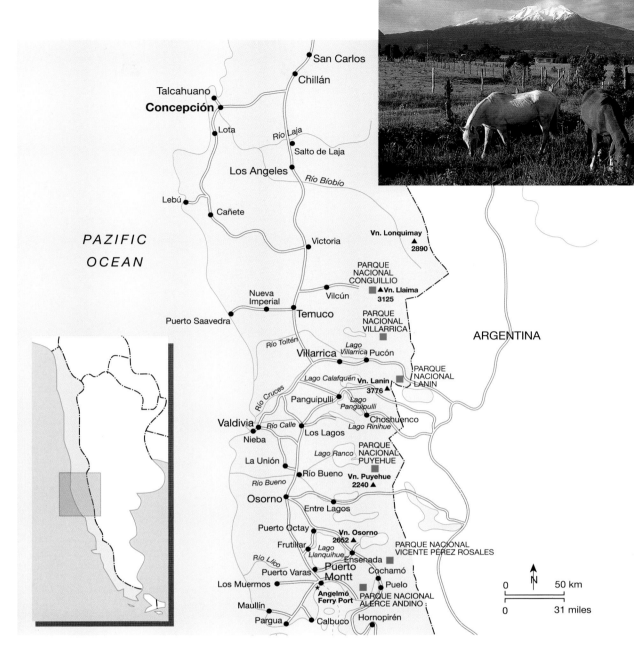

San Carlos
Chillán
Talcahuano
Concepción
Lota
Río Laja
Salto de Laja
Los Angeles
Río Bíobío
Lebú
Cañete
PAZIFIC
OCEAN
Victoria
Vn. Lonquimay
2890
PARQUE
NACIONAL
CONGUILLIO
Nueva
Imperial
Vilcún
Vn. Llaima
3125
PARQUE
NACIONAL
VILLARRICA
Puerto Saavedra
Temuco
ARGENTINA
Río Toltén
Lago
Villarrica
Villarrica
Pucón
PARQUE
NACIONAL
LANIN
Lago Calafquén
Vn. Lanin
3776
Río Cruces
Panguipulli
Lago
Panguipulli
Valdivia
Río Calle
Choshuenco
Lago Rinihue
Nieba
Los Lagos
PARQUE
NACIONAL
PUYEHUE
La Unión
Lago Ranco
Río Bueno
Río Bueno
Vn. Puyehue
2240
Osorno
Entre Lagos
Puerto Octay
Vn. Osorno
2652
Frutillar
Lago
Llanquihue
Río Llico
Ensenada
PARQUE NACIONAL
VICENTE PÉREZ ROSALES
Puerto Varas
Puerto
Montt
Cochamó
Los Muermos
Puelo
Angelmó
Ferry Port
PARQUE NACIONAL
ALERCE ANDINO
Maullín
Pargua
Calbuco
Hornopirén

0   N   50 km
0   31 miles

A rural idyll: Criollo horses belonging to the Mapuche graze in front of Calbuco Volcano (above). – A brightly colored wooden church in the Lake District (center). Mapuche children by Lago Llaniquihue (below).

Mapuche, who had fought so bravely against the Spanish colonial powers and were now being treated no better by the Chileans.

Orllie-Antoine contacted one of the Mapuche princes and had himself proclaimed King of Patagonia. To this day the Mapuche insist it was all wishful thinking. Why should a Frenchman be accepted as their ruler after rejecting the Spanish and the Chileans?

The Chileans also thought that the Périgord lawyer had simply gone too far. They saw it as a wooden horse ploy by the French Emperor with the goal to take possession of Chile and colonize it again. Orllie-Antoine was forced to leave the country several times, but he kept on saving up the money to pay for his passage back. He had a national anthem composed and stationery printed.

105

The story ended in tragedy, and the only original documents telling the fate of Orllie-Antoine "le 1er, Roi de la Patagonie" are to be found in the National Library in Santiago.

The Mapuche territory of those days must have been a fairy-tale land, a succession of dense forests, deep lakes, wild fuchsias, bamboo groves and a chain of snow-capped volcanoes. Their sacred tree, the acaucaria, is a deciduous conifer that casts a conical silhouette with spreading branches covered in jagged thick, brown scales. The Mapuche make flour from its cones. The finest examples are to be found in the Parque Nacional Conguillio, where, lined up in rows, the trees look like a succession of open umbrellas.

Today the land is entirely given up to agriculture. It is covered with fields intersected by roads occasionally interrupted by villages and towns. The original charms can still be experienced at

In the dense forests of the South the ground is often marshy, and logs make the pathways secure for driving cattle (left-hand page). Huasos gather for the rodeo in Cochamó (bottom left). – A woolen beret for chilly days (left). – This wooden house in Cochamó could also be in Germany (below).

the foot of the Andes, where the luxuriant natural vegetation has been preserved here in numerous National Parks.

But what of the Mapuche? Under the democratic governments succeeding Pinochet their land was returned to them. Not all of it, and not immediately. For the Mapuche, who have retained their pride and self-confidence despite their period of captivity the process is not progressing fast enough. Nonetheless, they have at least been able to retain their culture.

The Coal of Lota

A rags-to-riches story of the kind familiar in North America – and one which tells us a great deal about the social elite in Chile and their rise to prosperity. Matias Cousiño began his professional career in 1828 as a postman in Valparaíso before moving on to

cattle trading in Argentina. Later, relying on his good fortune as a businessman, he became involved in the silver mines at Chañarcillo near Copiapó in the Norte Chico.

Then coal deposits were discovered in Lota. The mines in the North and the steamships in Valparaíso harbor needed vast quantities of fuel. Since there was no wood in the deserts of Northern Chile, coal mining promised vast profits. Matias Cousiño changed jobs again. The coastal strip was confiscated from the Mapuche. They probably had no idea of the riches buried deep in the coastal mountains.

In any case, the Cousiño-Goyenecheas were a family of entrepreneurs who earned a fortune with the coal of Lota. Their reputation grew. The church in Lota is dedicated to San Matias. The entrepreneur's elaborate monogram could be seen everywhere. Soon it adorned the labels on the bottles from the Cousiño Macul vineyard, which the family also acquired and which today enjoys an international reputation. The family did not want to demonstrate its newly-acquired wealth in a workers' settlement. And so they engaged a French architect to build them a house in Santiago, at that time, the most magnificent residence in the capital.

An imposing rocky landscape rises up near Lota above a bay once inhabited by fishermen. The coal seams are buried deep within its interior. Since 2002 the state has been at the head of an attempt to revive Lota, whose mines were closed in 1997 causing many people to lose their livelihood. The plan is to have the little town gain a place on the tourist map. Former miners will guide visitors through the industrial architecture and the mines. Visitors who can understand Spanish will find it is a most interesting destination.

The Europeans are Coming

The journey continues southward, past the country's granaries around Angol and Chillán. As long ago as the 1840s the government decided to encourage European immigrants to settle the land of the Mapuche. Agents charged with attracting European immigrants began their work. They were especially successful in the smaller states of Germany, whose citizens had suffered under the failed revolution of 1848. There were political refugees, too, who came to live in a democratic country.

Two brothers from Kassel, in Germany, reaped great rewards at this time. One of them, Bernardo, explored the South, while Rudolph Amandus investigated the stony deserts of the North. Bernardo traveled as an agent for German colonization to the place where Puerto Montt now lies, and continued as far as Lake Llanquihue, which today provides the finest example of German-Chilean colonization. In those days the third-largest lake in South America was surrounded by dense jungle and marshy shores. During the course of this ambitious project the government had soon let all available plots of land to German immigrants.

They established their main base and trading center in the town of Osorno, 80 kilometers (50 miles) further north. They crossed the lake in boats, and soon there were some 40 moles jutting out into Lago Llanquihue. Some of them can still be seen today, and the pretty wooden villas built by the prospering families are regarded by the Chileans as being typical of their German heritage.

If you travel a short distance to the north of Osorno, you will reach the charming river port of Valdivia, which became the second center for German immigrants. Even today, Karl Anwandter's

Lake Llanquihue was one of the regions settled by German immigrants (above). – The German influence is much in evidence in the overall appearance of Puerto Octay and in the wooden houses of Ensenada (below), even in the small details: the sign outside the Kunstmann brewery in Valdivia (right-hand page, below). Opposite: Temuco is famous for its markets: the Fería Pinto is particularly colorful. The Mapuche from the surrounding villages meet every morning to trade their wares (above and center). – Also shown: a woman selling herbs in Puerto Varas and a fishmonger in Angelmó (below).

See page 114

Holidaymakers enjoy the summer weather at the foot of Villarrica Volcano.

Hiking, Riding, Water Sports

Leisure activities in Chile

1 Chile provides a wide variety of pastimes for sports enthusiasts. Things can get quite wet if you go river rafting on the Río Petrohue at the foot of Osorno Volcano. Cycling in Conguillio National Park. – 2 Canyoning is gaining increasing numbers of fans. If you dare, you can try it out on Lake Todos Los Santos. – 3 A tourist group climbs the sand dunes in the Valle de la Luna in to take in the sunset. – 4 Riding in Southern Chile is great fun.

The Andes, with salt flats on its high plains and glaciers, is a quite difficult but challenging terrain for hikers and trekkers. The region boasts the world's highest volcano, the Ojos de Salado, South America's highest peak, Aconcagua and the granite peaks in the Torres del Paine National Park.

If you crave a real test you can cycle up Licancabur volcano, which is approximately 6,000 meters (19,685 feet) high, or spend several days hiking across the glacier fields in the South. Less energetic, but still a challenge, is mountain-biking along the Carretera Austral, 1,200 kilometers (750 miles) in length and an ideal route for cyclists. There are also one-day hikes in the blazing sun along the salt flats at an altitude of almost 3,000 meters (9,842 feet). To visit the spot where, according to Darwin, even the Devil freezes in Hell – Cape Horn – you can join sailing trips lasting for several days. Canoeing fans will find rough seas in the fjords of the far South; if you feel chilly you can warm up afterwards in the thermal springs bordering some of the fjords.

The Indian expression "futaleu-fú" means "Great River" – "*Río Grande*". It extends south of Lago Yelcho as far as the Argentine border. It is popular among rafters and canoeists, as it offers the entire range and degree of difficulty. For

4

5

American and Canadian fly-fishermen the Far South is a great tip, particularly the Río Baker south of Lago General Carrera and Lago Cisnes near Villa O'Higgins.

There is a sporting activities tourist center at Puerto Varas on Lake Llanquihue and another in Pucón on Lago Villarrica. Through-out the region guest houses have language and sports courses on offer. You can also climb volcanoes, or go rafting, canoeing and riding. If you prefer to go riding in the North, you should visit the Hacienda Los Andes in the Valle Hurtado. Conaf, the national forestry commission, clears hiking trails through the nature reserves and national parks.

In the more popular tourist regions there is a dense network of paths. The creators of "Sendas de Chile" aim to establish footpaths across the entire length of the country. Some regions have made good progress with the project, and the individual stretches have a certain pioneer flair. The path around Lago O'Higgins at the end of the Carretera Austral is a case in point. In the Parque Nacional Puyehue, which is easily accessible from Osorno, there is a 25-kilometer (16-mile) sendero (path) to Casablanca Volcano. In the Norte Grande a lonely footpath crosses the Altiplano over a distance of 68 kilometers (43 miles) from the Salar de Huasco.

Watersports enthusiasts enjoy the coast near Iquique, with its good conditions for windsurfing. Or just go swimming if you prefer! That you can certainly do at the many lakes south of Santiago, a popular summer retreat.

You will find information under: www.azimut.cl

(sports, extreme sports); www.simltd.com

(Cape Horn, Tierra del Fuego), www.villaohiggins.cl (hiking at the

end of the Carretera Austral), www.haciendalosandes.com

(riding and hiking), www.aquamotion.com

(sports in the South), www.sendasdechile.cl

(Senderos de Chile), www.monatanamarchi-le.com

(sports and wine trips).

chemist's shop (see p. 116) enjoys a good reputation because he was not only the first person to import beer, but was also a pioneer in establishing Valdivia's reputation as a center for small-scale industry. By the end of the 19th century it was one of the best-developed towns in the country.

An Idyllic Setting

The region between Temuco and Puerto Montt is an idyllic landscape of lakes, forests and volcanoes. No wonder that, apart from

The araucaria (monkey-puzzle tree) is the most important plant of the Mapuche Indians. In fall they harvest the cones to make flour. In the Parque Nacional Conguillio (all photos) the araucaria is a protected tree. The tree's comical silhouette has earned it the nickname "umbrella" (paragua).

agriculture, clean industries are once again attracting interest in Southern Chile. There is much for tourists to see and do here: hiking, trekking, canoeing, climbing volcanoes, swimming in the volcanic lakes, riding, cycling, bathing in hot springs – and getting to know the culture of the Mapuche, visiting their restaurants, cultural centers, houses and historical museums. The gentle climate is reminiscent of central Europe and the Mediterranean.

The Lake District is currently one of the best-equipped regions of Chile for tourists, without being overcrowded. Near Temuco, the bizarrely attractive landscape surrounding the volca-noes of Lonquimay and Llaima is home to a National Park and three nature reserves. The most popular holiday locations, including the odd five-star hotel, are concentrated along Lake Villarrica, 130 kilometers (81 miles) southeast of Temuco. Villarrica is gradually losing its somewhat rustic character, while Pucón, at the foot of the beautiful volcano of the same name, has enjoyed its starring role for somewhat longer. Pedestrian areas, comfortable hotels and wooden chalet-style villas, as well as shops selling chocolate and cafés, all give the town a European flair. There are thermal baths on Lago Villarrica and somewhat more rustic examples near Coñaripe and Liquiñe.

Along the Bandits' Trail

Puerto Varas, which lies on Lago Llanquihue, is just as international and youthful as Pucón. It is from here that Mathias Holz-

Rise and fall: the numerous eruptions of Llaima Volcano have left their mark on the appearance of Conguillio National Park (above). – The most recent eruption destroyed the forests by Laguna Verde (below).

mann and Lex Fautsch give their guests a send off into the Andes. They provide them with horses and food for the journey, which will follows the route taken by Butch Cassidy and the Sundance Kid, the most famous bank robbers of all time.

The two bandits had settled down to breed cattle in Cholila in Argentina. They used false names to purchase land in the Patagonian Andes. The inhabitants of Cholila, some of whose grandparents had known the outlaws maintain that the famous cowboys were friendly and helpful neighbors. They even financed the construction of a log road across the border to Chile.

We traveled along this road on horseback, once used for driving cattle. It leads through dense, cool temperate forests with a

particular form of vegetation known as the Valdivian cloud forest. The *arrayanes, pitra, roble, lenga* and *coihue* trees grow so close together the branches and crowns form a shady dome. Frequent rainfall makes it a mud bath and so it requires the wooden logs to make it traversable.

It is extremely narrow, having barely enough width to accommodate cattle walking two abreast. The stretch running to La Junta follows the course of the Río Cochamo like a picturesque little mountain meadow, complete with wild flowers. A pass cuts through the snow-capped mountains to Argentina. The land of the Mapuche really is exceptionally beautiful.

117

A lonely world of water and land: near Cochamó.

"A Rotten Trunk, what a treasure..."

Wild, strange, full of secrets: the forests of Chile

4

3

1 Light southern beech forests in Torres del Paine National Park. The lichens grow on araucarias. Traces of slash-and-burn beside the Carretera Austral. – 2 In fall, the colors of the forest on Tierra del Fuego are at their most attractive. 3 The ancient kenua forests grow at an altitude of 4,000 meters (13,123 feet) in Isluga National Park. – 4 Southern shrubs blossoming in the forest in Queulat. 5 A parasitic plant in the shrubs around Lago Pehoe.

The poet Pablo Neruda described it best: "Beneath the volcanoes, at the foot of snow-capped mountains, between the great lakes – the fragrant, wild Chilean forest. ... Further on, I walk through a forest of ferns which are far taller than I am: sixty tears fall from their cold, green eyes onto my face, and their fan-shaped leaves beneath me tremble after I have passed ... A rotten trunk, what a treasure; black and blue fungi have given it ears; red parasitic plants have sowed rubies across its surface ... " A remarkable variety of species does indeed grow here. In the Puyehue National Park near Osorno alone you will find some 700 classified species of plant in the evergreen wet forest. The *ar-*

2

rayanes, with their conspicuous cinnamon-colored bark and its light markings, are thought to lower the temperature. For the Mapuche the araucaria tree is both useful and sacred. As far south as the Torres del Paine National Park in South Chile you will find south-

ern beeches, magnolias, and species of cypress, hazelnut, elms and laurel trees. In the Valdivian

6

7

5

cloud forest there are also tree ferns, groves of bamboo, fuchsias (the copihue, the national flower, is also a species of fuchsia), cinnamon trees and oaks.

It surrounds the Seno de Reloncavi and appears in the Fray Jorge National Park, not far from dry La Serena, thanks to the coastal fogs. Many of the flowers which bloom here have only local names. The wealth of flora here is simply incomparable.

This excess encouraged over-exploitation. For decades, wood remained one of the country's most important export items. Trees were felled thoughtlessly, and entire regions suffered great erosion as a result. You can see the results on Easter Island, which was reforested with eucalyptus, and on the Isla de Chiloé, where at first sight the pine forests serve as replacement for the original cover of valuable woods. But fast-growing pine trees and eucalyptus serve at best to anchor the slopes and prevent further erosion of soil which has already been washed away. The imported wood species lower the quality of the soil and prevent the formation of humus. And, of course, the wood is not as valuable as the original Chilean species.

In the meantime, the government has learned from its mistakes and is adopting a more sensible reforestation plan, such as that around Coyhaique. It was a foreigner, however, who voiced concern about the forestry reserves long before all the post-Pinochet governments. More than a decade ago, Douglas Tompkins, a North American, bought the first forests of alerce (Patagonian cypress) trees around Fjordo Reñihue to save them from being felled. Here, the slow-growing alerce can live for over 1,000 years. It has spread steadily southwards.

With his Parque Pumalín, Tompkins polarized the entire country. However the dispute is settled; let us explore the Chilean forests! There are many places to go; near Cochamó, Pucón, near Puerto Fuy, Llanquihue or Choshuenco. For, as Pablo Neruda maintained, those who do not know the forest "do not know the planet".

121

Gold, Sheep and Ice

The Challenges of the South

The Isla de Chiloé America's second-largest island after Cuba, is only 20 minutes by boat from the mainland. It presents a completely new aspect of the widely contrasting landscapes in the country. If you compare the Carretera Austral, which begins at the same latitude, to a romantic opera, then the island would be a quiet drama. Geographically speaking the island is part of South Chile, but it must be treated as a separate entity.

The most prominent scent on the Isla de Chiloé is the smell of smoke. Every market square is enveloped by it, even the countless packets of dried seaweed and the chains of dried red shells dangling like necklaces from the stalls. It escapes from the packets of smoked meat on the butchers' stalls and from the market restaurants where they serve the island's traditional dish, smoked pork or curanto, simmering in huge pots. For generations, the islanders have preserved their food by smoking it.

Salmon versus Seafood

The beauties of Southern Chile: the vast, deep-blue expanse of Lago General Carrera; an enchanted southern beech forest by the Rio Grey (above) and a waterfall in the green inferno of the Parque Nacional Queulat (right-hand page).

Traditionally, the inhabitants of the Isla de Chiloé lived principally on seafood. Here it is not just a matter of distinguishing between a cockle and a mussel; so many varieties of shellfish are found here that Hector, the owner of the market restaurant "El Sacho de Ancud" in Dalcahue cannot even list them all: *cholgas, choros, machas, locos, choros zapato, picarocas, piure, almejas, navajas, percebes…* They are eaten raw or at least immediately after being caught; anything which cannot be eaten at once will be smoked and used to make a soup during the winter.

Along the Carretera Austral you will find places full of enchantment; the "Hotel Termas de Puyuhuapi" is just one of them (above); the azure blue icebergs in Lake Grey (center) are another. The little girl is the daughter of German immigrants (right). – The endless skies above the steppes of Southern Patagonia (right-hand page, top). – Timber determines the routine of everyday life in Caleta Tortel (right-hand page, below).

Flying across the island you can see that the entire coastline surrounding the gently rolling green interior, with its countless bays and headlands, is full of breeding basins for salmon. Salmon, however, are not a native species of Chile; they have been imported and are produced in vast numbers. Chile is now the world's second-largest salmon exporter. But salmon spoil the natural living conditions of the shellfish, whose number and quality is being continually reduced. The salmon is forcing the shellfish out of existence; for the island inhabitants, that is more or less as if the Chileans were to expel the Chilotes. Their relationship to each other was never particularly good.

For a long time, the Chileans dismissed Chiloé as backward, poor and inhabited by illiterates. This verdict may reflect the fact that Chiloé remained loyal to Spain after the rest of the country had shaken off the colonial power. Until 1826, the Royalists were able to take refuge here in spite of the fact that Chile had declared independence in 1818. Apart from the fishing industry no other useful industry was established. Instead, they more or less deforested the island. Whatever is not protected by the National Parks or Nature Reserves consists mainly of tree plantations of little value.

Chiloé also exported labour. The Chilotes are said to be particularly reliable and tenacious. They were employed in the carpet factory in Puerto Puyuhuapi and as lumberjacks in Caleta Tortel.

Chiloé has its own story of the creation, its own myths and sagas, its own repertoire of fairies, long-haired sorceresses, virile gnomes and evil ghost ships. In these stories, Chile does not even exist.

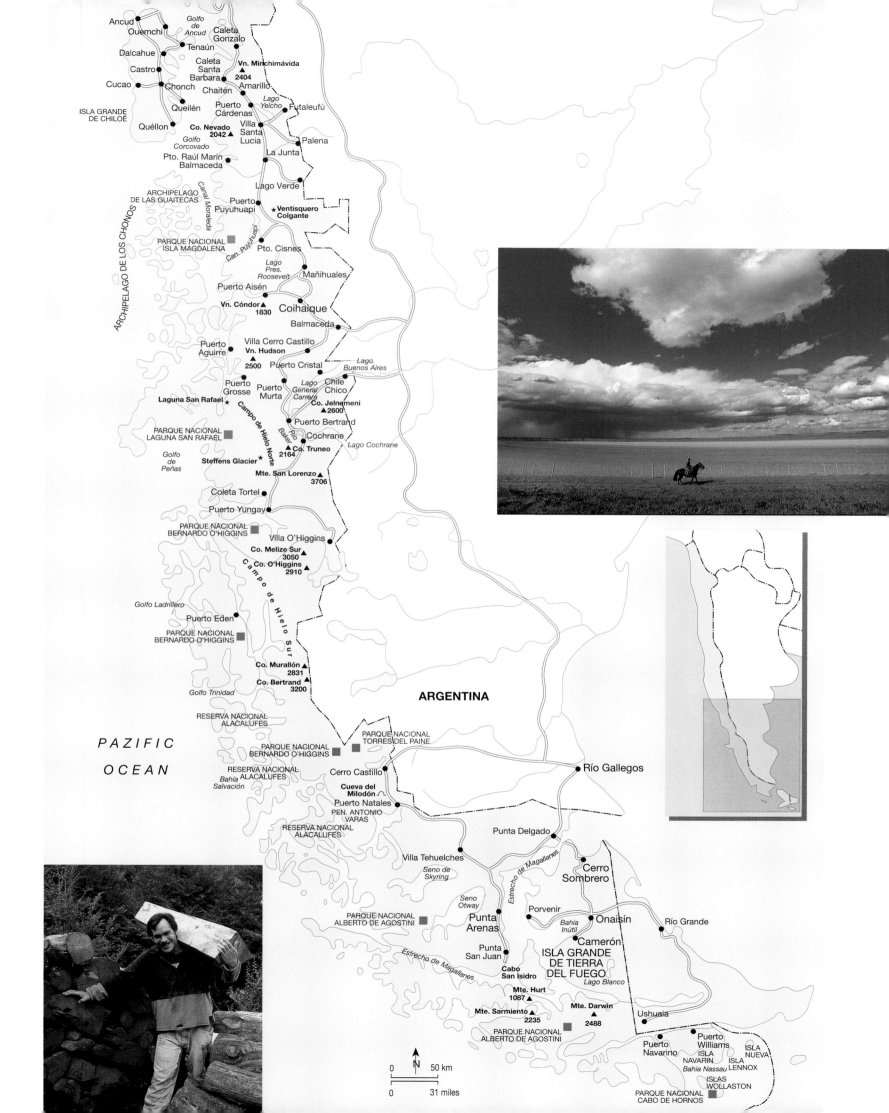

Ancud
Quemchi
Golfo de Ancud
Caleta Gonzalo
Dalcahue
Tenaún
Caleta Santa Barbara
Vn. Minchimávida
▲ 2404
Castro
Chaitén
Amarillo
Cucao
Chonch
Puerto Cárdenas
Lago Yelcho
Futaleufú
Queilén
Villa Santa Lucia
Palena
ISLA GRANDE DE CHILOÉ
Quéllon
Co. Nevado
2042 ▲
La Junta
Golfo Corcovado
Pto. Raúl Marín Balmaceda
Lago Verde
ARCHIPELAGO DE LAS GUAITECAS
Puerto Puyuhuapi
★ **Ventisquero Colgante**
Canal Moraleda
PARQUE NACIONAL ISLA MAGDALENA
Pto. Cisnes
Can. Puyuhuapi
Lago Pres. Roosevelt
Mañihuales
Puerto Aisén
ARCHIPELAGO DE LOS CHONOS
Vn. Cóndor ▲
1830
Coihaique
Balmaceda
Villa Cerro Castillo
Puerto Aguirre
Vn. Hudson
▲ 2500
Puerto Cristal
Lago Buenos Aires
Puerto Grosse
Puerto Murta
Lago General Carrera
Chile Chico
Laguna San Rafael ★
Campo de Hielo Norte
Río Baker
Co. Jelnemeni
▲ 2600
Puerto Bertrand
Cochrane
PARQUE NACIONAL LAGUNA SAN RAFAEL
Lago Cochrane
Co. Truneo ▲
2164
Golfo de Peñas
Steffens Glacier ★
Mte. San Lorenzo ▲
3706
Coleta Tortel
Puerto Yungay
PARQUE NACIONAL BERNARDO O'HIGGINS
Villa O'Higgins
Co. Melize Sur ▲
3050
Co. O'Higgins ▲
2910
Golfo Ladrillero
Campo de Hielo Sur
Puerto Eden
PARQUE NACIONAL BERNARDO O'HIGGINS
Co. Murallón ▲
2831
Co. Bertrand ▲
3200
Golfo Trinidad
ARGENTINA
RESERVA NACIONAL ALACALUFES
PARQUE NACIONAL TORRES DEL PAINE
PAZIFIC
OCEAN
PARQUE NACIONAL BERNARDO O'HIGGINS
RESERVA NACIONAL ALACALUFES
Cerro Castillo
Río Gallegos
Bahía Salvación
Cueva del Milodón
Puerto Natales
PEN. ANTONIO VARAS
RESERVA NACIONAL ALACALUFES
Punta Delgado
Villa Tehuelches
Seno de Skyring
Estrecho de Magallanes
Cerro Sombrero
Seno Otway
Porvenir
Onaisín
PARQUE NACIONAL ALBERTO DE AGOSTINI
Bahía Inútil
Río Grande
Punta Arenas
Punta San Juan
Camerón
ISLA GRANDE DE TIERRA DEL FUEGO
Estrecho de Magallanes
Lago Blanco
Cabo San Isidro
Mte. Hurt
1087 ▲
Mte. Darwin ▲
2488
Ushuaia
Mte. Sarmiento ▲ 2235
PARQUE NACIONAL ALBERTO DE AGOSTINI
Puerto Navarino
Puerto Williams
ISLA NAVARIN
ISLA NUEVA
Bahía Nassau
ISLA LENNOX
ISLAS WOLLASTON
PARQUE NACIONAL CABO DE HORNOS

0   50 km
N
0   31 miles

Along the Carretera Austral, a farmer's life is not always easy. It is certainly lonely. The villages are widely scattered. The dense forests were cleared in many places to make way for grazing land and agriculture. Farmhouses in Puyuhuapi (above), herding the cattle on a hacienda east of Cochrane (right) and a huaso with a yoke of oxen near Futaleufú (right-hand page, top).

126

The Salesian Museum in Punta Arenas

Gliding above the visitors' heads is the skeleton of an antediluvian flying lizard. The Museo Regional Salesiano in Punta Arenas is a treasure chest of astonishing exhibits and a very unusual local-history museum. Here are to be seen not just the findings of scientists but also interesting contributions from sailors and gold-diggers. On the ground floor there is a collection of animals which live in Southern Chile, comprising a large number of birds, seals, guanacos and rodents. Arrow tips, projectiles and hand-axes are displayed in glass cases and they have even reproduced the interior of a cave to create a more whole impression. It was the Salesian monks who took care of the Indians, protecting them from persecution and saving them from being hunted by the sheep barons. They also documented what happened. On the first floor there are photos of the execution gangs commissioned by the landowners and then prints of the numerous relief institutions the Saleisans established which were equipped with schools, kitchens and sewing rooms.

The idiosyncratic mixture of independence, a fairy-tale world and the beauties of nature appealed to Chilean hippies. Suddenly a community of velvet-clad individuals appeared on the island with sleeping bags. The Chilotes are a trusting lot, and the tourists from the mainland, most of them very young, were welcomed warmly. Open-air concerts and cinema now take place on the central square in Ancud.

Adventure along the Carretera Austral

Across on the mainland, however, the landscape offers a dramatic combination of glaciers, glacial lakes and rivers, slopes and hanging bridges, as well as wooden bridges, waterfalls, dense forests, deep valleys and windy *meseta*. The region is virtually uninhabited, and what few towns there are have been established or developed to any significance only over recent decades. Lonely farmsteads and cattle farms are tucked away behind avenues of

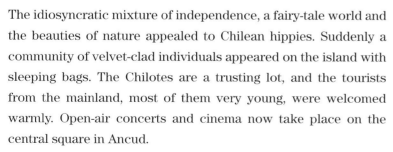

*The Isla de Chiloé forms its own minia-
ture universe. The tourist attractions
include the houses on stilts and the interior of the wooden church in Castro
(above and right). – The islanders meet
for the procession in Achao (below).*

poplars and forests of *arrayán* (myrtle) trees. From time to time
you may meet a *pilchero*, the Chilean gaucho, a mounted cattle
driver with his dog, or an occasional mountain biker or bus. Otherwise the solitude is total.

Since 1986 the Carretera Austral has led from Chaitén past
these natural sights. The construction of the road began under
the military dictatorship of Augusto Pinochet. In 2000 the road
was extended to Villa O'Higgins and in 2004 the most recent
branch leads to Caleta Tortel. Many other branches are planned
or already under construction. At present the road is 1,200 kilometers (750 miles) long.

Looking at the road, you can appreciate the difficulties which
had to be overcome during the course of this mammoth project.
South of Chaitén the coastal fjords cut deep into the interior. The
entire region is dominated by glaciers and intersected by rivers.
Along the roadside, wooden signposts recall the names of the
roadworkers killed during its construction. The plan is for Carretera Austral to extend as far as Puerto Natales. Then the main

links will be complete in a region which was virtually uninhabited at the beginning of the 20th century.

At the end of the 19th century expeditions were also sent to the deep South. Amongst the leaders of such expeditions was Hans Steffen, a German, who named a valley near the present provincial capital Coyhaique "Kaiser Wilhelm", Valle Emperador Guillermo. A few pioneers also decided to settle here. They were followed by settlement companies, mostly from Argentina, as it was easier to develop the land from there. They felled as many trees as they could. Throughout the entire far South, vast scars left by the felling and burning of trees serve as a reminder of what happened. For the development companies the felling of the valuable trees – hardwood alerce, cypresses, laurel trees, oaks and southern beech – brought in large profits as vast amounts of the wood were required for railway sleepers. Later it was in great demand all over the world.

To create pasture and agricultural land even the first settlers set fire to the forests. Axes were useless against the mighty trees.

See page 134

129

Lichen forests in fall near Puerto Natales.

The Screaming Stones

The Torres del Paine National Park

1

2

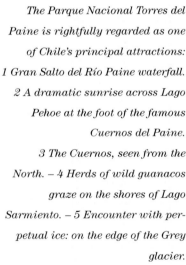

3

The Parque Nacional Torres del Paine is rightfully regarded as one of Chile's principal attractions: 1 Gran Salto del Río Paine waterfall. 2 A dramatic sunrise across Lago Pehoe at the foot of the famous Cuernos del Paine. 3 The Cuernos, seen from the North. – 4 Herds of wild guanacos graze on the shores of Lago Sarmiento. – 5 Encounter with perpetual ice: on the edge of the Grey glacier.

Gazing at the jagged granite peaks of the Torres del Paine massif, you find yourself searching your mind for a suitable metaphor. The Tehuelche were the first to describe them poetically; they called them "The Screaming Stones". Today we perhaps would describe them as forks of lightning embedded in the ground and then turned to stone. Or that they are like a sprawling, abandoned fairy castle. Even seasoned mountaineers, who have scaled peaks the world over, declare it is the most dramatic mountain panorama in the world, concentrated in the smallest area.

We took our seats on the bus in Puerto Natales early in the morning for the ride to the National Park. It is about 120 kilometers (75 miles) away, and is one of Chile's main tourist attractions a

must for anyone visiting the country. The area preceding it is dead flat and windy, in brief, pretty unspectacular. One minute the sun may be shining brightly then suddenly hailstones whip across the road cutting through the vast sheep-farming region. The climate here is typified by rapidly changing weather patterns.

The tension was mounting. We had been promised views long before

we would reach the Park. And then, on the far horizon, we suddenly caught a glimpse of the barely visible granite summits of the Cuernos del Paine, snow lying between the jagged peaks. Our great anticipation had not been in vain.

The three massifs are made up of granite, limestone and volcanic layers. Ancient glaciers cut and ground the *cuernos* (horns) and *torres* (towers), topping them with

4

5

jagged peaks and carving out deep indentations making them dramatically resemble the spine of a dragon. Tongues of the glacier, sparkling with crystals of ice, lie between the cracks in the rock filled with debris. The massif is reflected in Lago Pehoe, which gleams in shades of green or blue depending on the sun's rays. Someone described the mountains as a gift and it seems an appropriate way of regarding them.

Over the last few years the Parque Nacional Torres del Paine has become increasingly popular. All who visit Chile hope they will make the drive through at least once. There is an abundance of sights to see in its 242,000 hectares (600,000 acres). Wild guanacos, small wild camels, charge along across the steppes while *bandurrias*, *gaganchos* and various species of wild duck forage for food in the lakes. Daisies, violets, china orchids and deadly nightshade carpet the steppes in delicate and bold beauty. Forests of *ñire* give off their strong honey-like aroma.

Originally inhabited by the Tehuelche, the immigrants used it as pasture land. Only one example of a cattle farm has survived here – transformed into a *hostería* to cater for the influx of visitors.

The varied landscape of lakes, waterfalls, alpine meadows, mountains and glaciers is crisscrossed by trails, footpaths and steep tracks. The choice of excursion is determined by the individual's skills and by the climatic conditions – it can be very windy and the rain can squall almost horizontally. The Grey glacier spreads picturesquely into the park, and the lake is dotted with icebergs.

Climbers from all over the world feel the challenge of the vertical peaks of the Torres del Paine for they present some of the most difficult climbing anywhere on the planet.

133

The fires raged uncontrolled and without hindrance, at Lago General Carrera, for instance they blaze lasted three long years.

Parque Pumalín: Wilderness for Sale

It was not a Chilean but a North American who took it upon himself to protect the forests and thus to retain the country's green lung. Douglas Tompkins of San Francisco, co-founder of the textile companies Esprit and North Face, has been buying land in Chile since 1992. By now his Pumalín project encompasses the alerce woods of Hornopirén, and the Reñihue Fjord as far as the volcano Michinmáhuida. For years he has been fighting to have his project recognized as a National Park. The longer the struggle continues, the more embittered it becomes – and the more confusing the arguments on each side sound. For some he is an eco-terrorist; for others, the most important environmental protector in the entire country. Some people maintain that the Chileans should be ashamed that no one of their own has achieved as much. In Chaitén, at least, Douglas Tompkins is a hero.

134

In 1936 two Germans called Hopperdietzel and Grosse founded Puerto Puyuhuapi together with two other immigrants. The village lies in a no man's land of fjords, tree ferns and glaciers. The textile engineers established a carpet factory which is still operating today – 13 women from Chiloé work at the weaving frames. Señor Hopperdietzel junior produces from his jacket pocket a card with the internet address. The carpets can be ordered from anywhere in the world. An incredible fact to consider when strolling through a village in which time appears to have stood still, everything seems cozy – but poor.

The atmosphere has a hint of the Wild West. The few villages between the grandiose landscape of volcanoes and lakes seem to have a defiant, pioneer quality about them. They shelter in the lee of the biting winds, like Puerto Ibáñez beside the bright blue waters of Lago General Carrera, the second-largest lake in South America (the largest is the Lago de Titicaca); some are crowded together under a proud collection of corrugated-iron roofs such as Villa Cerro Castillo; others yet again look a bit neglected, like Puerto Guadal. But everywhere, as in charming Caleta Tortel or in Villa O'Higgins, they radiate a warm hospitality – probably because the inhabitants like living here and are pleased to welcome guests. And so the gangs of road workers continue to blast the rock in order to extend the Carretera Austral as far as Puerto Natales. A few decades ago it was thought that extinct prehistoric creatures could be found here; today it is the site of one of Chile's most attractive National Parks, Torres del Paine. Puerto Natales is the ideal place to begin exploring it.

Wide, Open Sheep Country

Chile's southernmost point faces Tierra del Fuego. In this area they sent and confined mentally ill people who had committed a crime. A single lonely fort represents Chile's claims to the coast along the Magellan Strait. During the 1880s three families bought up vast tracts of land in the region and set up sheep farms.

José Nogueira, Maria Behety, and Sara and Mauricio Braun-Menéndez established their empire on several million hectares of land. The vast profits they made enabled them to import every imaginable luxury to Punta Arenas from velvet curtains and English prints to antiques and precious crystal. They resided in villas

with conservatories, and amused themselves attending balls and going to the opera. People from the North are amazed, after being used to the sight of simple windswept cottages, suddenly to be confronted with elegant stone houses.

The sheep barons, however, turned their land into a vast prison for the nomadic Tehuelche and Selk'nam. They accused the Indians of stealing their animals. The Chilean government did not intervene so the Indians became human booty; their hunters were unhindered acting without fear of punishment for their acts. The latter were often former gold prospectors down on their luck and were charged with chasing away – and if necessary killing – the Indians. The only safety afforded the Indians was in the Salesian monasteries.

Southern Chile is a world of ice and water: you can explore the Grey glacier by boat (left-hand page), as well as the icebergs in the Beagle Channel (center) and the marble cathedrals near Puerto Tranquilo on Lago General Carrera (above).

Tierra del Fuego, the End of the World

The mole at Porvenir stretches out into the sea. Black-necked swans swim out to greet the ferries from Punta Arenas, a safe harbor on legendary Tierra del Fuego. Today there are no reminders of the Wild West and the Gold Rush: just a church, a museum and tubs of flowers on the central square. The little museum recalls the first settlers from Croatia as well as the Selk'nam, and shows photos of them digging for gold. Those who came to Tierra del Fuego hoped to find gold or work on the sheep farms which were largely owned by Scottish immigrants. In the mid-19th century to the beginning of the

20th century many seal and whale hunters sailed across the Southern Ocean. To the present day evidence is to be found in many locations in the form of oil pots and the remains of hunted creatures. Such memories are kept alive in Puerto Williams, the most southerly town in the world, surrounded by magnificent forests at the foot of the granite peaks of the Dientes de Navarino massif. In its museum celebrated photos by the Wroclaw missionary Martin Gusinde are on exhibition. Gusinde had been the only white man permitted to observe and photograph the rites of the Selk'nam. The main attraction after Puerto Williams lies a few hundred kilometers further south: Cape Horn, where according to Darwin even the Devil freezes in Hell. Now, at long last, you have arrived at *el fin del mundo*, the end of the world.

Untrodden paths: there are only wooden landing stages and stairways in Caleta Tortel (above). – Magellan's penguins inhabit the coast of the Seno Otway (center). White and shining and still largely unexplored, the Darwin Cordillera rises above the Beagle Channel (right).

World's End: the Río Baker near Cochrane.

Welcome to the Countryside

Accommodation in unusual hotels

1 and 4 An oasis in the Norte Chico: the "Hacienda de los Andes" in the Valle Hurtado. It combines in attractive manner the styles of Spain and Tuscany: terracotta, tiles, flowers and seashells as a substitute for gravel. – 2 Very popular: an osteria in Pisco Elqui.

3 Minimalist and cool: the "Terrantai" is an adobe hotel in San Pedro de Atacama which was built using only local materials.

5 The hotel "Termas de Puyuhuapi" offers thermal pools between tree ferns and fuchsias.

In a country with such magnificent natural settings, the most unusual hotels are to be found away from the main cities and roads. An excellent example is the hotel "Termas de Puyuhuapi" by the fjord of the same name. Accessible only by ferry it is surprising to find such a comfortable spa hotel with excellent cuisine south of the quaint but remote village of Puerto Puyuhuapi on the Carretera Austral.

The elegant wood and glass building extends along a black gravel beach. You can sit outside in the steaming hot springs in the shade of nalca bushes, ferns and copihue shrubs, enjoying the view across the fjord. One of the most exciting excursions is the trip to see the

4

5

calving glaciers in the Laguna San Rafael.

On the shores of Lake Risopatrón near Puerto Puyuhuapi are the wooden villas of the "Hostería El Pangue", which also offer a range of extremely attractive excursions.

Sports form a major part of the activities in the "Terra Luna Lodge" by Lago General Carrera near Puerto Guadal. Philippe Reuter, the owner, has spent many days walking across glaciers or cycling up volcanoes and you can book similar excursions in his lodge. Or you can spend your days lazing beside the lake. The main hobby of Señor Christensen at the "Mallín

Colorado" is birdwatching. The family, of Danish origin, also have comfortable wooden houses for accommodation set in a large garden estate beside Lago General Carrera.

You will have to search hard to find the "Hacienda Los Andes". The mansion and its extension on the banks of the Río Hurtado retain the elegant style of former estates. Manuela Paradeiser and Clark Stede's main hobby is breeding horses, so riding is part of the standard program here. If you prefer to go hiking you will not be sent off on a wild goose chase. They themselves have designed the hiking program.

Planning your Journey

Size/Location/Geography

Chile shares a border with Peru in the North and with Bolivia in the Northeast. Its Pacific coast is 6,435 kilometers (4,021 miles) long; it shares the cordillera of the Andes in the East with Argentina. The land area totals 756,096 square kilometers (291,853 square miles) including Easter Island and the four islands of the

A cactus stands sentinel above the pass in the Elqui Valley.

Juan Fernández archipelago and the uninhabited islands of Seca and Gómez. It is a land of contrasts. In the North is the Atacama, the world's driest desert, and

The Caleta Portales between Valparaíso and Viña del Mar.

down in the far south, the indented coast forms the Campo de Hielo Sur, the largest single field of ice between the Caribbean and the Antarctic. Two parallel mountain ranges divide Chile along almost its entire length: the volcanic Andes and the coastal mountains which the Pacific then divides into a labyrinth of islands and channels south of Puerto Montt. Between the mountains is the Valle Longitudinal, the longitudinal valley. This central region is characterized by fertile basins and hills.

The country's regions are dubbed the Norte Grande, the Norte Chico, the Central Region, the South and the Far South.

Flora and Fauna

The Aymara, who live between the Andean peaks of the Norte Grande, plant corn, oregano, olives, quínoa, onions, carrots, garlic and potatoes at high altitudes. Away from the small fields given over to agriculture you will see candelabra and pillar cactus, low-growing lichens and thorny bushes. Flamingoes stalk across the high-altitude marshes and local ducks and rare moorhens swim in the pools. This is the natural habitat for llamas, alpacas and vicuñas.

Towards the south, the vegetation becomes denser and taller. Winter rain causes the wild flowers and herbs to blossom in the Norte Chico. The little islands off the coast near La Serena are interesting for the Reserva Humboldt, where seals, penguins and seabirds are protected. Here, too, you will find one of only three colonies of dolphins in the entire world.

Central and Southern Chile is condor territory. Deep in the south you will come across colonies of penguins (Isla de Magdalena near Punta Arenas), seals, the ñandú (the "ostrich of the Pampas"), black-necked swans and guanacos. Dense forests once covered the entire region south of Concepción, but timber is Chile's main export. Elms, oaks, larches, arrayane and southern beeches are shredded to wood

In Fray Jorge National Park, a UNESCO biosphere reserve.

144

Climate in Santiago de Chile

Monthly average temperatures

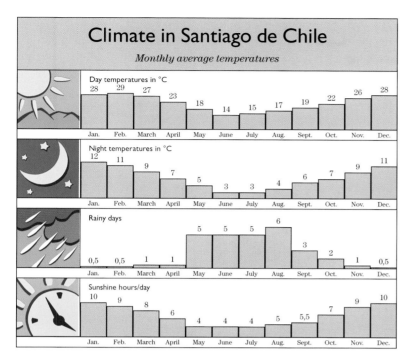

Day temperatures in °C

Jan.	Feb.	March	April	May	June	July	Aug.	Sept.	Oct.	Nov.	Dec.
28	29	27	23	18	14	15	17	19	22	26	28

Night temperatures in °C

Jan.	Feb.	March	April	May	June	July	Aug.	Sept.	Oct.	Nov.	Dec.
12	11	9	7	5	3	3	4	6	7	9	11

Rainy days

Jan.	Feb.	March	April	May	June	July	Aug.	Sept.	Oct.	Nov.	Dec.
0,5	0,5	1	1	5	5	5	6	3	2	1	0,5

Sunshine hours/day

Jan.	Feb.	March	April	May	June	July	Aug.	Sept.	Oct.	Nov.	Dec.
10	9	8	6	4	4	4	5	5,5	7	9	10

chips before being loaded onto freight ships for Japan and Canada. The alerce (Fitzroy cypress) is now protected and environmental problems are being addressed, not least because the forested regions in the south are important as potential tourist destinations.

The Pacific breakers gently lap at the crescent-shaped beach at Zapallar.

Climate/Best Time to Visit

Chile stretches over a length of 4,329 kilometers (2,705 miles) and 39 degrees of latitude, corresponding to the distance between Norway and the Sahara. The large number of different climatic zones and landscapes make it possible to visit the country at any time of year. Chileans themselves like to travel between mid-December and mid-March, so the hotels in tourist destinations are likely to be full. If you want to visit the Torres del Paine National Park during this season, for instance, you should book well in advance. Northern Chile can be visited all the year round; for the south, the months between October and March are ideal as long as you don't plan a skiing holiday. The temperatures vary depending on altitude and proximity to the

Skiing in the Andes at Portillo.

sea. In the north the climate is hot and dry, whilst in the south it tends to be cool and windy. Central Chile has a pleasant, almost Mediterranean climate. In general the temperature differences between day and night tend to be extreme. In the Atacama Desert the swing can be as much as 30 degrees. Between June and October it is relatively cool in Santiago and further south and there is snow in the Andes.

Easter Island is around 3,800 kilometers (2,375 miles) from the mainland and has a completely different climate. Average temperatures are between 24 °C (75 °F) in January and 18 °C (64 °F) in July. Should you be planning to visit the entire country the best time to travel is between the end of September and April.

Public Holidays and Religious Festivals

1 January – New Year (Año Nuevo)

Easter (Pascua). Easter Monday is not a holiday.

1 May – Labor Day (Día del Obrero)

21 May – Navy Day; anniversary of the Battle of Iquique 1879

29 June – Saints Peter and Paul (San Pedro y San Pablo)

15 August – Assumption of the Virgin (Asunción)

18 September – Independence Day (Día de la Independencia)

12 October – Columbus Day (Día de la Raza)

1 November – All Saints' Day (Todos los Santos)

8 December – Immaculate Conception (Immaculada Concepción)

25 December – Christmas (Navidad). Christmas Eve is an official working day; Boxing Day is not celebrated.

Archaic figures still play a role in the Festival of the Virgin in Aiquina.

Arrival /Visas

At present it is not possible to fly from Europe to Santiago non-stop. Flights to Chile from Europe take at least 17 hours. A flight from London via Buenos Aires to Santiago lasts 13 hours, from New York via Buenos Aires to Santiago about 14 hours, from Washington D.C. to Santiago non-stop 12 hours and from Los Angeles to Santiago non-stop 16 hours.

To visit Chile as a tourist, in most cases you will only need a valid passport. (Europeans as well as citizens of Australia, New Zealand, Japan, South Africa). When entering the country you will receive a Tourist Card issued by the International Police (at no cost), which is valid for a period of 90 days. The Tourist Card must be returned when leaving the country.

Citizens of the USA and Canada have to pay for a tourist visa. Further information: Extranjería, Moneda 1342, Santiago, Tel. 0056/2/6705320 www.embajadaconsuladoschile.de

World's End: Hanga Roa airport on Easter Island.

At the Mercado Fluvial in Valdivia.

Health/Medical Care

There are good health facilities in Santiago and the other major cities, but private clinics/hospitals are expensive. We recommend that you obtain comprehensive travel and medical insurance before traveling.

In March 2007, the World Health Organisation confirmed reports of dengue fever in Chile. There is no effective treatment for dengue, which has severe flu-like symptoms and can sometimes be fatal in the elderly or the very young. You are advised to check on local conditions when traveling within Chile and to minimize exposure to mosquito bites by covering up and using repellents. Air pollution in Santiago during winter (June-September) is a major problem. There are sporadic cases of cholera outside Santiago. Typhoid and hepatitis are fairly common, especially during the warm season, which lasts from December to March in Central Chile. Chemist's shops (farmacías) often sell cosmetics and drugstore articles. A sign labeled "turno" lists details of 24-hour, night and weekend duty rotas.

Information

The state tourist information office Sernatur, www.sernatur.cl, has offices in all regional capitals and many other towns in addition to its headquarters in Santiago. A large selection of brochures is available.

Turistel is one of the most comprehensive guides to Chile. It also has an English website: www.turistel.cl

You can also find information and tips on the website of Lan, the Chilean national airline: www.lan-chile.com.

Further information: www.embassyworld.com/ embassy/Chile www.visit-chile.org www.gochile.cl

Swimming

The cool Humboldt Current prevents temperatures in the most popular Pacific seaside resorts in Central Chile, such as Viña del Mar, Reñaca and La Serena, from rising above 20–21 oC (68-70 oF). In the south the sea is too cold for

Limestone formation near Iquique.

swimming. The temperatures in Iquique and Arica are suitable for bathing virtually all the year round.

The Lake District in the South also has a succession of attractive lakeside resorts. The lava beach bordering Lake Villarrica in Pucón is very popular, as are Caburgua and Lakes Calafquén and Llanquihue and the resorts of Puerto Varas and Frutillar.

Shopping

For some years, Santiago has prided itself on offering the most expensive, largest and most modern shopping centers in the whole of South America. Galerías and

On the Road

Through Chile with a Camper

The steaming waterspouts of the Tatio geysers shoot like red flames into the purple evening sky of the Altiplano. Then the black of night descends over the high-altitude valley, 4,500 meters (14,764 feet) above sea level. There is no sign of human habitation – apart from us. And we can witness the spectacle only because we are traveling in a camper. It would be too dangerous to drive to the nearest hotel, and too cold to spend the night in a tent.

Chile is rich in places where the magic is only accessible to those who spend the night there. No one residing in hotels will experience the pinkish-red thunderstorm of thousands of flamingos rising heavenwards in the morning sun

by the Salar de Surire, or see the sunrise above the Pacific mist by the Pan de Azúcar, or bask in the morning calm of the myrtle forest of Lago Rieco.

For some years now, those who find tents too damp, too cold or too uncomfortable have the alternative of exploring the country in a

camper (Holiday Rent Campers Santiago). Apart from the major cities and their environs, Chile is a very safe destination for visitors in camping buses. There is a dense network of campsites (Turistel camping guide) and plenty of places in the countryside where you can spend the night. The tried and tested rule of all campers applies here too – leave nothing but

your footprints. Rangers are becoming increasingly annoyed at the garbage left behind by campers. If you abide by the handful of sensible rules, however, in Chile you can experience journeys in a camper which for decades

have no longer been possible in densely populated Europe.

Arriving at Pan de Azúcar National Park (above) and a welcome break at the picnic area on the beach (left) and in the Parque Nacional Fray Jorge (left). – A suspension bridge by Lago General Carrera (below).

147

Natural Beauty

The most interesting National Parks

1 In Lauca National Park, with Parinacota Volcano on the horizon. – 2 Blossoming cactuses in Fray Jorge National Park. 3 The Information Center in Queulat National Park. – 4 Tall trees in Conquillio National Park. – 5 A finch. – 6 Armadilloes inhabit the entire region of South Patagonia. 7 A zorro colorado or desert fox, in the Pan de Azúcar National Park.

As soon as we reached Lago Chungará, 4,517 meters (14,819 feet) above sea level in Northern Chile, we set off to explore the enchanting landscape. The deep-blue waters reflect the peaks of the surrounding volcanoes. It is best to walk slowly in the thin mountain air, otherwise one is likely to lose one's balance.

There was perfect peace on all sides. Lago Chungará, the highest volcanic lake in the world, is like a picture postcard, surrounded as it is by the rust-colored summits of mountain peaks soaring to 6,000 meters. It is located in Lauca National Park, one of 31 throughout the country. The Parque Nacional Lauca was created in 1970. It includes the folds of the Cordilleras and the Altiplano, across whose

brown steppes dotted with high-altitude marshland the snow-capped volcanoes of Parinacota, Pomerape, Guallatiri and Acotango rise heavenwards. Conaf, the state-run forestry authority, has laid out refuges and footpaths.

To enter Volcán Isluga National Park, further south, you can drive through Lauca Park via Guallatiri along a hair-raising gravel road as far as Enquelga. You can stay overnight in the Conaf refuges or in the simple guesthouses in Colchane.

The Tres Cruces National Park is no busier. Salt pans, dark green lagoons, sulfur mines and mountain formations which look as if they have been drawn by a magician's hand permit only sparse vegetation. Flamingos feed in the icy wa-

ters of the mountain lakes. One of them, the Laguna Verde, is the site of the base camp for those planning to climb the Ojos del Salado, the highest mountain in Chile (6,893 meters/ 22,615 feet).

In order to explore all the varied facets of nature which Chile has to offer, you should visit one of the National Parks in the South – for example, the 250,000-hectare (617,500 acre) Parque Nacional

6

7

4

5

Vicente Pérez Rosales. It was named after the first agent who recruited immigrants from Europe. From the shores of Lago Llanquihue, where the German immigrants settled, the park spreads out like a delta towards the Argentine border. Some of the scenic highlights include the volcanoes Osorno and Puntiagudo, as well as Lake Todos Los Santos. The Lake District was once covered in dense jungle; to-

day it is well cared-for and accessible via numerous paths. A popular excursion tour, the "Cruce de los Lagos", links Chile with Argentina across the lake plateau.

The southern part of the country suffered badly from deforestation during the 20th century and happily large tracts of land have recently been placed under a conservation order. One National Park follows the next along the Carretera Aus-

tral. The Parque Nacional Queulat attracts visitors with the hanging glaciers which give it its name. You can reach them on foot and by boat. When the region was explored during the 19th century to determine what resources it offered it had never previously been settled.

A pioneer gave his name to one of the islands: Robinson Crusoe, aka Alexander Selkirk, who served as

the model for Daniel Defoe's famous mutineer, who was actually cast away here, some 360 miles from the coast.

The only villages on the archipelago, consisting of just three islands, lie where the sailor's fateful story was played out – without his imaginary companion Friday, as it happens.

Robinson Crusoe Island has been described by scientists as a Noah's Ark for threatened species, since it is the habitat of rare plants, many of them found only here. Palm trees, myrtle, cinnamon trees, tree ferns and orange trees as well as the sandalwood tree, a native of Polynesia, flourish in the volcanic soil.

Not all the pollens and plants have been identified and catalogued. Some of the footpaths laid out by Conaf weave their way across the Archipiélago Juan Fernández National Park.

149

shopping arcades are the most popular meeting places in the cities.

The less well-off meet on the ferias persas – literally, the "Persian Markets". The food markets are worth visiting. The Mercado Municipal in the capital has become a

cas – in Temuco and Pucón. Woolen goods and cowhide bags in Coyhaique. Carvings made in liparite, a white volcanic stone, are to be found in Toconao. Lapis lazuli and moonstone are typical precious stones in Chile.

The best places are: Santiago,

The pedestrian zone of Arica, Chile's northern most town (above). – Driving donkeys in the Altiplano. Such scenes have become rare in Northern Chile (above, center).

popular tourist attraction. The market at Temuco is one of the town's main sights. Other interesting food markets are the Feria Pinto in Temuco, the Feria Modelo in Calama, the Mercado Fluvial in Valdivia and the Angelmó fish market in Puerto Montt. You can buy local crafts at markets or in specialist shops. Wood carvings on Easter Island. Knitted items and baskets in Castro, Dalcahue, Ancud, Achao and Quellón (Isla de Chiloé) and in Puerto Montt/Angelmó. Jewelry made by the Mapuche Indians – also repli-

Hard work for meager wages: a Mapuche woman weaving a carpet in Puyuhuapi.

Pueblito Los Domínicos, it is laid out like a little village featuring 180 cottages where potters, artists, metalworkers, tailors and women knitting are all to be seen hard at their task. Nearby is a 17th-century church. In Arica is the Pueblo Artesanal, a crafts-

men's village on the way to the Valle de Azapa.

Getting Around

The roads throughout the country are in good or excellent condition, and are patrolled by cara-

bineros. The Carretera Austral is mostly made of gravel and soil, as are the smaller roads and side roads, especially in the Andes in the North. Due to the long distances involved many visitors choose to fly. The routes are shared between Lan Chile – which also offers an air pass which can only be purchased abroad before the start of the journey, www.lanchile.com – and Ladeco and National Airlines. In the far South small airlines also operate: Aerochaitén, Alpine Air and DAP www.dap.com. Lan Chile flies to Easter Island, and you can reach the Isla Robinson Crusoe (Fernández) via TAIRC.

Santiago has a modern underground which runs throughout

An old German steamship in Valdivia harbor.

www.chileinfo.de. The services run more frequently during the summer months. It is advisable to book as soon as possible if traveling on popular routes such as the Carretera Austral or from the Isla de Chiloé towards the South or from Puerto Montt to Puerto Natales: www.tranmarchilay.cl and www.navimag.cl.

Icebergs often make landing difficult at Refugio Grey. This is the starting point for many hikes through the National Park.

Cruises on the waterways of Patagonia and to Laguna San Rafael: www.patagoniaconnection. cl and www.skorpios.cl; Antarctic cruises will be found under www.crucerosaustralis.cl.

Health precautions

No specific vaccinations are prescribed for visitors to Chile. Nonetheless it is advisable to consider protection against tetanus, typhoid and hepatitis A and B. It is recommended that you carry a vaccination certificate amongst

your travel documents as it also indicates your blood group. Even on cloudy days it is advisable to use a sun cream with a high protection factor.

Museums

Like many countries in the world, the museums in Chile are usually closed on Mondays. On Sundays they are often only open until the early afternoon.

Safety

Tourists are treated courteously and respectfully. You will not normally be cheated by taxi drivers, attacked at bus stations or have your belongings stolen from your hotel room. Women traveling alone especially appreciate this fact.

It is nonetheless advisable to take certain precautions and keep large quantities of cash and valuable jewelry in the hotel safe. Have your documents close to you but do not take them with you if you go for a walk at night.

the city from 6 a.m. until 11 p.m. Metrobuses are to be found waiting at the ends of the lines. There is a shuttle bus linking Merino Benítez airport with the center of Santiago.

The bus companies are private and generally offer a good service. If you plan to travel long distances by bus you should book one of the comfortable reclining seats. In the South, where the coast is deeply indented, you will often need to take the ferry. Prochile provides addresses and information on its website

Discovering Chile

The Five Most Scenic Routes

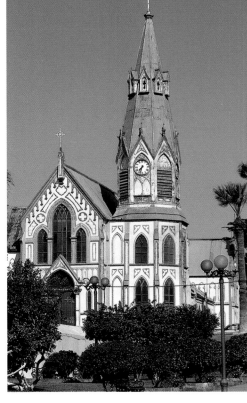

Gustave Eiffel built the church in Arica

I. Along the Carretera Austral

Good planning and plenty of time are essential for the Carretera Austral. Chaitén is dominated by the

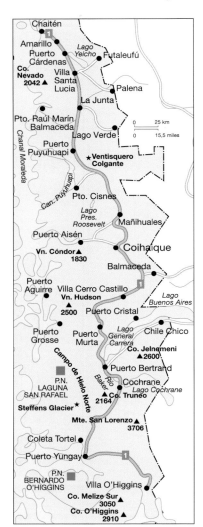

volcanoes Corcovado and Michinmahuida. Yelcho Lake and Glacier are the first highlights. The pioneer town of Villa Santa Lucía is sur-

rounded by meseta beyond which is a fairy-tale forest with tree ferns, alerces, southern beeches and groves of bamboo. Leave enough time to visit the hanging glacier of Queulat near old-fashioned Puerto Puyuhuapi.

The road goes on towards Coyhaique, the provincial capital. Then you are not far away from Lago General Carrera, the second-largest lake in South America, and its beautiful bays of intense blue and green.

When the Hudson volcano erupted in 1990, entire tracts of land disappeared under a layer of ash. Lake Carrera flows into Río Baker, whose numerous rapids make it a fly-fishing paradise. Take a detour to Caleta Tortel. The little pioneer town Villa O'Higgins marks the end of the Carretera Austral.

Spring by Lago General Carrera.

II. From Arica to Lauca National Park

Our goal, Arica, is 4,600 meters (15,000 feet) above sea level. The section of the route up to the Altiplano is attractive for its changing scenery and traces of Indian culture. The canyon of the Río Lluta is given over to alfalfa fields and cattle farming. On the mountainsides

you can see huge geoglyphs dating from 1000 B.C., representing animals, people and cult symbols. One of the oldest churches in the region is the Iglesia de San Geronimo in

Poconchile. The Pukara Copaquilla dates from the 12th century, followed by the Tambo de Zapahuira, a rest and news station on the old Inca Path. The putre, lying at 3,500 meters (11,483 feet), had old Indian predecessors, as did archaic Parinacota, a staging post on the trading route between Arica and Potosí. The emerald green Lago Chungará in Lauca National Park lies amid snow-capped volcanoes.

III. From San Pedro de Atacama to Calama

You will have to get up at 4 a.m. to see all the highlights along the route. The first is the Tatio geysers at an altitude of 4,300 meters (14,100 feet), which the rising sun rouses to life. Then take the turnoff to the aerodrome, after 14 kilometers (9 miles) turn right at the crossroads. The road is impassable after rain. When you reach the Cuesta Chita the landscape opens up, rendering lovely views of the

Río Loa. In little Toconce the terraced fields are a sight to behold. Make a detour to the Pukará de

Turi. After 41 kilometers (26 miles) the road surface improves considerably. The Indio village of Caspana appears and you can climb down to visit the village museum

Adobe church in Chiu-Chiu.

and St Luke's Church. The pilgrimage town of Ayquina is a remarkable phenomenon. It only wakes up on festival days in honor of the Virgin Mary. A scenic road leads down into the colonial town of Chiu-Chiu. The stretch as far as Calama is asphalted.

IV. Through the Land of the Mapuche

Forest roads wind between lakes and volcanoes through what was once Mapuche territory. From Villarrica, on the lake of the same name, the road continues through fertile woodland to the resort of Lican Ray on the shores of Lago Calafquén and then follows the black-sand shoreline towards Coñaripe.

The stretch along the Cuesta Los Añiques has picturesque views of volcanoes and Lake Pellaifa. There are a number of spas in the vicinity. The road winds its way through oak and beechwoods down to Lago

Neltume and on to Choshuenco, a farming community, and to the timber port of Puerto Fuy on Lago Pirihueico. There is a lovely short walk

Araucarias near Lanin Volcano.

Castro, with its famous wooden cathedral, is the capital of the Isla de Chiloé.

to Huilohuilo waterfall. The view of the conical Choshuenco Volcano accompanies the route beside Lago Panguipulli into its namesake town. In Riñihue you will find lovely beaches and a comfortable hotel.

V. On the Isla de Chiloé

The first stop on the idyllic island with its farms and fishermen's cottages is Caulín, for its restaurant specializing in oysters. The colorful port of Ancud cascades down a succession of terraces towards the sea. Here – as with all other places mentioned – you should visit the market and the museum.

The road leads downhill through a deforested area towards Dalcahue, a port of embarcation for the little archipelago off the coast, where you can see some of the wooden churches built by Franciscan

monks. Castro, the capital of the island, attracts visitors with its typical stilted buildings. Chonch is one of the prettiest villages on the island, and the scene of an annual farmer's market which draws many

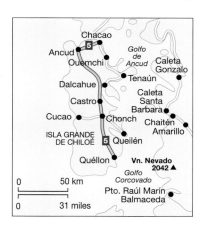

visitors. Traveling west you will reach Chiloé National Park, with its dense forests of alerce, cinnamon trees and southern beeches. To the south lies the end of the island and Quéllon, the export harbor for seafood.

153

Post/Internet

The Chilean postal service is reliable; a letter or postcard does not normally take longer than ten days to reach central Europe. The poste restante system (lista de correos) works reliably and well. A letter or postcard to an overseas destination costs 210 pesos. Internet cafés have sprung up in the larger towns as well as in university cities and tourist destinations.

Telephone

Overseas mobile telephones (in Chile: cellular) usually do not work in Chile. Please check your provider website for more information. Bellsouth rents mobile phones at Santiago airport. Even in the smallest town you will find a centro de llamadas, a telephone office for international calls. You can purchase a card for a telephone cabin.

Calls connected via the hotel switchboard are considerably more expensive. The country code for Chile is 0056.

Tipping

Restaurant bills are usually rounded up to an extra ten percent. In hotels chambermaids, garage attendants and bellboys will also expect a tip.

Self-catering cottages near Refugio Grey (above). – Luxurious accommodation in Torres del Paine National Park: "Osteria Pehue" lies by the lake of the same name (main picture). Colonial buildings surround a little square in Arica (right).

Accommodation

A wide range in accommodation of all categories is available in the capital, and the standard corresponds with European norms. You can also find inexpensive rooms. Family-run guesthouses are known as *hospedajes* and *residen-*

ciales; they provide an alternative to the smaller hotels, for example in Pucón, Puerto Varas, Puerto

Octay, Villarrica, Caracautin, Puerto Natales, Punta Arenas and San Pedro de Atacama.

other currencies in the exchange booths (casas de cambio) in Santiago. Some are also open on Saturdays.

Banks which are designated "Redbanc" have ATMs (cajeros automáticos).

On Easter Island the Banco del Estado de Chile will only change US dollars until 12 noon. Dollars are accepted as the second official currency. It is not possible to

The barman in Café Brighton in Valparaíso preparing the national drink, pisco sour (left). – Bars line the streets of Bellavista, the artists' quarter of Santiago (top right).

Currency

The Chilean Peso (CLP) circulates in coins of 1, 10, 50 and 100 pesos and in notes to the value of 500, 1,000, 2,000, 5,000 and 10,000 pesos. The current exchange rate is approx.: 1 Euro = 722 CLP, 1 US Dollar = 590 CLP.

US dollars are the easiest currency to change; it is better to change

draw cash using a credit card here. ATMs are widely available. Credit cards (Visa, Mastercard and, to a lesser extent, American Express) are accepted in most large shops and hotels. Dollar travelers' checks are more widely accepted than travelers' checks in other currencies. Larger hotels will also change money, but at a less favorable rate.

Time Difference

The time difference between local Chilean time and GMT/ BST

and CET varies according to summer and winter. From the second Saturday in October until the end of March the difference between Chile and the U.K. is minus 3 hours; between Chile and Europe it is minus four hours. From the second Saturday in April until the end of September the time difference is five hours (U.K.) and six hours (Europe). During the two weeks between the dates when

the clocks are changed in Europe and in Chile (End of September until the second Saturday in October, and end of March until second Saturday in April) the time difference is four hours (U.K.) and five hours (Europe).

Customs

Items required for personal use during the journey and your stay in Chile may be imported free of duty. There are no restrictions on the import and export of foreign currencies.

155

People, Places, General Expressions

Huasos in Torres del Paine National Park

Reflections of the cathedral in Santiago

Pelicans in the port at Arica

Flowing over the lava: Petrohue Falls

A detail at Hacienda de los Andes

A grill restaurant in Antofagasta

Right-hand page:
The famous granite needles of
Torres del Paine

Moai on Easter Island

Credits and Imprint

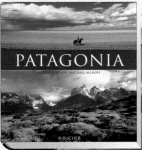

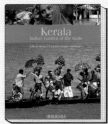

The photographer

Hubert Stadler (1054–2005) was a freelance photographer who specializes in South America and Northern Europe. He has published numerous albums of photographs, articles and travel reports in national and international magazines. He was a member of Corbis photo agency.

The author

Susanne Asal studied history, ethnology and English. Since 1986 she has worked as a freelance travel journalist. She lived for several years in Mexico and Argentina. She is the author of numerous illustrated books and travel guides, especially on the Spanish-speaking world. She lives in Frankfurt am Main.

Cover photos:

Front cover: Gaucho at the "Hacienda de los Andes (left); lichens on Parinacota Volcano in Lauca National Park (right).
Back cover: Santiago de Chile.
P.1: A Mapuche Indian woman's market stall in Parinacota.
P.3: Mask at the Festival of the Virgin in Aiquina (top), llamas in the Altiplano (bottom).

Text credits

The quotations on page 12, 33 and 120 are by Pablo Neruda. © 1984–86 by the heirs of Pablo Neruda., translated by Jane Michael.
The text "On the Road: Through Chile with a Camper" was written by Hubert Stadler.

Photo credits

Archiv für Kunst und Geschichte, Berlin: p. 22/23
Bildarchiv Preußischer Kulturbesitz, Berlin: p. 22/23 bottom, 23 bottom and center
ESO, Garching: p. 68/69 left and bottom, 68/9, 69 right
Interfoto, Munich: p. 20 center
Keystone/ Studio X, Limours: p. 22 bottom
Picture Alliance/ dpa, Frankfurt: p. 20 bottom, 21 bottom (2) and top right
Sotheby's/ Archiv für Kunst und Geschichte, Berlin: p. 23 top
All other photos are by Hubert Stadler, ©Sylvia Scholpp-Stadler, Fürstenfeldbruck, Germany

This work has been carefully researched by the author and kept up to date as well as checked by the publisher for coherence. However, the publishing house can assume no liability for the accuracy of the data contained herein.

We are always grateful for suggestions and advice. Please send your comments to:
C.J. Bucher Publishing,
Product Management
Innsbrucker Ring 15
81673 Munich, Germany
E-mail: editorial@bucher-publishing.com
www.bucher-publishing.com

Translation: Jane Michael, Munich, Germany
Proofreading: James Rumball, Hamburg, Germany
Graphic design: graphitecture book, Rosenheim, Germany, revised by Wiebke Hengst, Ostfildern, Germany
Cartography: Astrid Fischer-Leitl, Munich, Germany
Product management for the German edition: Joachim Hellmuth
Product management for the English edition: Dr. Birgit Kneip
Production: Bettina Schippel
Repro: Repro Ludwig, Zell am See, Austria
Printed in Slovenia by MKT Print